A Tale

A new town, a new h...

Best friends Grace and Jenni have sworn off romance. They adore bringing little miracles into the world, but their jobs as midwives are as close to love and babies as they're going to get. Until fate leads them across the globe and straight into the arms of the men who'll change everything...

Falling for Her Forbidden Flatmate

Living with her best friend's brother might not be ideal, but after a difficult divorce, a fresh start in New Zealand is just what Grace needs. What she could do without is the undeniable chemistry between her and gorgeous obstetrician Jock... Giving in to their attraction would be a terrible idea. But will she be able to resist her roommate?

Miracle Twins to Heal Them

On the last night of her trip to visit Grace and Jock, Jenni finds herself alone with deliciously handsome anesthetist Dan. But what was supposed to be a vacation fling becomes oh-so-complicated when she discovers that she's pregnant—with *twins*!

Both available now!

Dear Reader,

I was born and bred and now live in the South Island of New Zealand, and we like to call ourselves the Mainlanders ;-) In an amazing country overall, the South Island has more than its fair share of attractions and, if you're ever lucky enough to get here, don't miss the top. The Marlborough Sounds are stunning and that's where my twin siblings—Jock, the hero of *Falling for Her Forbidden Flatmate*, and Jenni, the heroine of *Miracle Twins to Heal Them*—end up living.

Their shared childhood had scarred them both badly enough that they were in danger of missing out on the best that life can offer—true love.

Fortunately, Grace and Dan come into their lives, and it's not just the scenery that will take their breath away.

Happy reading.

With love,

Alison xxx

MIRACLE TWINS TO HEAL THEM

ALISON ROBERTS

MEDICAL ROMANCE

H Harlequin®
MEDICAL ROMANCE

Recycling programs for this product may not exist in your area.

ISBN-13: 978-1-335-94257-9

Miracle Twins to Heal Them

Copyright © 2024 by Alison Roberts

Harlequin Enterprises ULC
22 Adelaide St. West, 41st Floor
Toronto, Ontario M5H 4E3, Canada
www.Harlequin.com

Printed in U.S.A.

Alison Roberts has been lucky enough to live in the South of France for several years recently but is now back in her home country of New Zealand. She is also lucky enough to write for the Harlequin Medical Romance line. A primary school teacher in a former life, she later became a qualified paramedic. She loves to travel and dance, drink champagne, and spend time with her daughter and her friends. Alison is the author of over one hundred books!

Books by Alison Roberts

Harlequin Medical Romance

A Tale of Two Midwives

Falling for Her Forbidden Flatmate

Daredevil Doctors

Forbidden Nights with the Paramedic
Rebel Doctor's Baby Surprise

Morgan Family Medics

Secret Son to Change His Life
How to Rescue the Heart Doctor

Paramedics and Pups

The Italian, His Pup and Me

Fling with the Doc Next Door
Healed by a Mistletoe Kiss
Therapy Pup to Heal the Surgeon

**Praise for
Alison Roberts**

"The love story is built up slowly but surely with just
the right amount of passion and tenderness. This
novel will tug at your heartstrings and give you hope
in miracles. All romance readers need to grab a copy
of this terrific tale ASAP."

—*Harlequin Junkie* on
A Paramedic to Change Her Life

PROLOGUE

LIKE ANY GOOD fairy tale—or fantasy—there was a moment when everything changed.

Alice fell down the rabbit hole.

Cinderella's fairy godmother appeared.

Sleeping Beauty got kissed.

And Jenni McKay found herself unexpectedly alone with a tall, dark and very handsome stranger by the name of Daniel Walker.

Really tall. At five foot seven, Jenni had never considered herself to be short but the top of her head was barely level with Dan's shoulder.

Really dark too. He had pitch-black wavy hair and eyes as dark as sin. Even his skin was a rich, warm shade of olive brown.

And *so* handsome. It hadn't escaped Jenni's attention when she'd first clapped eyes on him earlier this evening that Dan Walker was quite possibly the most gorgeous man she'd ever seen in her life.

And the sexiest, she decided when they were well into the dinner party they were both attending.

Maybe it was those eyes.

Or the facial hair that made him look more than a little wild despite being so neatly trimmed.

It might have been, at least partly, due to his moodiness. Judging by his reluctance to chat to a stranger even though she was his best friend's sister and currently sitting beside him at this table in the restaurant, Daniel clearly hadn't really wanted to be invited to this gathering. Jenni had done her best by breaking the silence more than once.

'So how long did you say you've been living here?' she asked.

'Couple of years now.'

'What made you choose Picton?'

'Job came up.' The succinct tone discouraged any further curiosity. 'I needed a change.'

That was intriguing. A change from what? A place? A situation? A *woman*…?

Being mysterious added another layer to that sexiness but that trait paled in comparison to something that didn't become apparent until much later that evening, when they were alone.

A connection like nothing Jenni had ever experienced before.

Ever…

Probably the last thing either of them had expected that night was to end up alone with each other.

It had been Jock's idea to have a party to celebrate the last night of Jenni's visit to New Zealand before she headed home to the other side of the world. He and Grace—who'd become Jenni's best friend when they'd done their midwifery training together in Glasgow—were trying to persuade Jenni to consider coming to work with them in the obstetric department of the local hospital and they'd thought that introducing her to some of the people she could be working with might just tip the balance.

Jenni wasn't averse to the idea of a working holiday. The move had clearly been exactly the right thing for Grace to have done. Like Dan, her friend had been in need of a change too.

But had Dan also been attracted to this small seaside town on the tip of the South Island of New Zealand because it felt so safe?

Ironically, as it turned out, it had been Jenni who had decided Dan the anaesthetist should be invited tonight. For Grace's sake. She wanted her best friend to be as happy as possible, after all, and developing a friendship that might even turn into something more was not a bad idea. She'd also instructed Jock to invite his latest girlfriend, who turned out to be Mandy the ultrasound technician and she'd been the one to suggest that a date needed to be found for herself, so she didn't end up feeling like a fifth wheel at her own party, which was why Stefano, one of the ED doctors, had come along.

But who knew that Stefano and Mandy would be so attracted to each other? Or that this Brazilian restaurant would have a live band playing on a Saturday night and that both Stefano and Mandy were into Latin dancing? So there they were as soon as the main course was finished, slow dancing what looked like a rumba, their bodies close and gazes locked on each other's. They were already having a party all of their own.

And then the phone call came. Jock was being called back to the hospital for a woman who was seven months' pregnant and had been involved in a car accident. The serious complication of a placental abruption was a possibility and it turned out Grace was the woman's midwife so, of course, she had to go as well. They didn't know how long they might be gone but the plan became to meet up later at the cocktail bar Jenni had wanted to go to after the meal at this restaurant.

It was Dan who'd ridden in like a valiant knight on his white horse.

'Don't worry,' he said. 'I'll look after Jenni.'

It wasn't a problem.

Dan was more than happy to take responsibility for getting Jock's sister back home safely after their night out as a group fell apart at the seams.

Why wouldn't he be? Jenni McKay's fiery red hair, the freckles on her nose and her bright blue eyes made her the female version of his colleague and fishing buddy who'd become the closest friend he'd ever made as an adult. He felt almost as comfortable in Jenni's company as he would have been going out for a drink with Jock.

Except that she talked a lot more than Jock did. And Jock's hair didn't fall in shiny waves to his shoulders and he would never wear such a pretty summery dress, so this was distinctly disconcerting on more than one level.

'Have you found something you fancy?' he asked.

Jenni looked over the top of the cocktail bar's menu.

'A black margarita sounds interesting. I didn't know that black sugar even existed.'

Dan found the image of the drink. 'It's not a silly idea,' he said. 'To put something normally used to soak up toxins, like activated charcoal, into a drink that contains four different types of alcohol. It sounds lethal.'

'It looks lethal.' Jenni didn't sound unhappy about that. 'What are you going to have?'

'Espresso martini.'

'Classic.'

'There's a reason things become classics. And coffee after dinner is always good.'

'But only after dessert.' Jenni was looking at the menu again. 'I'll have one after the…tiramisu cocktail.'

A man bumped Dan's shoulder just as he was about to pick up the cocktails they'd ordered.

'Sorry, mate.'

'No problem. Didn't spill a drop.'

'Why don't you watch where you're going?' The woman with the man sounded completely fed up. 'Oh, wait…you never think about anyone other than yourself, do you?'

'Why don't you give me a break?' the man countered wearily. 'We're supposed to be celebrating our wedding anniversary.'

The woman's voice faded. 'Yeah…*right*…'

As he turned away from the bar, Dan caught the way Jenni's eyes widened. She leaned towards him. 'I'm so glad I'm single,' she whispered.

'Me too.' Dan held the glasses high to keep them out of harm's way. 'Shall we go outside into the garden? Looks quieter out there.'

They found an empty table in the corner of the courtyard. Jenni raised her glass to his.

'Here's to *never* getting married,' she said.

Her grin had the same kind of cheeky charm as Jock's. The smile that never failed to win a woman over. Who would have guessed that it could work on men as well?

Most men anyway. Dan was immune.

'Here's to never getting married *again*,' he said.

Jenni gasped. 'You've been married?'

'Just the once.'

'And you thought that was a *good* idea?'

Dan couldn't help the smile that was tilting his lips. 'It's okay. I know better now.'

He touched his glass to hers and they shared a glance as they both took their first sip.

A kindred spirit, that was what Jenni was.

An hour and a couple of cocktails later and it was becoming apparent that Jock and Grace weren't likely to join them, but it didn't matter any longer. He and Jenni were having a competition to come up with the best reason why it was so much better to be single.

'You can eat whatever you like, *when*ever you like.'

Dan had to agree. 'Reheated pizza at two o'clock in the morning can be good.'

'As much garlic as you want because nobody's going to complain about your bad breath.'

'Nobody's going to tell me off for getting home late if I happen to feel like a game of squash after work.'

'I get to choose what side of the bed I sleep on.' That wide smile was lighting up Jenni's face again. 'Sometimes, I sleep on *both* sides. Like a starfish.'

That stopped him.

Maybe those espresso martinis were stronger than usual. Because Dan was getting an image of Jenni McKay as a starfish on her bed and…it was doing strange things to his gut.

And his head. He had the odd thought that he could tell Jenni anything. Things that he'd never said to anyone else. He didn't normally say much to anyone, actually, so it was astonishing to hear the words that were coming out of his mouth right now.

'It's safer,' he said softly. 'You have to trust someone to make a relationship work, but if you trust someone who tells you lies you give them the power to destroy you.'

Jenni finished the last of her espresso martini. 'Oh, I hear you,' she said with deep feeling. 'Why is it that some people never learn that? My mother, for example, kept falling in love. Time after time. Even when we were kids, Jock and I thought it was stupid. We knew it was going to crash and burn. When we were thirteen we made a vow that we were never going to get married or have kids.'

'That one's not a problem for me,' Dan said. 'I can't have kids.'

'Why not?'

It was weird that he wasn't bothered by such a personal question. Even weirder that he didn't hesitate to respond.

'Bad case of mumps when I was kid. I got told that I had more chance of winning the lottery than getting anyone pregnant.'

Jenni had gone very still. 'I'm sorry,' she said. 'It's not fair having a choice taken away from you.'

The empathy was as disconcerting as everything else about this woman. Surprising.

Captivating...

'Nobody said life was fair,' he growled. 'But at least it should be honest.'

'I gave up believing in Santa when I was five years old,' Jenni admitted. 'And I guess I gave up believing in happy endings when I was thirteen.'

'Fool me once, shame on you,' Dan quoted. *'Fool me twice, shame on me.'*

There was no smile on Jenni's face now. Her gaze was locked on his. 'I can't abide lies,' she said softly.

Dan couldn't break that eye contact. It felt like there was an undercurrent of silent communication going on here.

Maybe it wasn't just the caffeine in his cocktails that was making every cell in his body feel so very wide awake.

'Neither can I,' he responded. 'If you can't trust someone, they're not worth knowing.'

'I *never* lie,' Jenni said.

Dan could believe that. Maybe he *wanted* to believe that? He took a sharp breath. This was getting entirely too heavy on both the obvious and the hidden levels. He needed to break what felt like a strangely intimate connection, even though he still couldn't look away from her eyes.

He smiled slowly. 'How do I know *that's* not a lie?'

'You don't.' Jenni was smiling back at him. The sexiest smile he'd ever seen. 'But does it matter?' she said softly. 'We're never going to see each other again, are we?'

That strange sensation in Dan's gut was suddenly recognisable. The magic words had been said aloud, hadn't they? The mantra that made it safe. A holiday fling. A casual encounter with someone passing through town. Someone he was never going to see again.

'That might be one of the best things about being single,' he said.

He could see the tip of Jenni's tongue as she touched it to her bottom lip. 'Are you talking about what I think you're talking about?'

Dan held her gaze but lowered his voice. 'It gets more intriguing, doesn't it? Knowing you're never going to see that person again.'

'And when it's never going to get spoiled by finding out that the second time isn't as good?'

She looked at his empty glass. 'Fancy another one?'

'No,' he said softly. He was sitting close enough to reach up and touch Jenni's cheek. To trace the line of her jaw with his forefinger until it reached her chin—ready to tilt it so that he could cover her lips with his own—because he could see the answer to his unspoken question in her eyes.

'I fancy *you*…'

Maybe Jenni hadn't recognised the significance of the moment that changed everything when she'd found herself alone with Dan.

But she couldn't miss the moment she began to fall into the sexual fantasy that was suddenly coming to life.

The moment she let Dan kiss her.

The moment she kissed him back…

CHAPTER ONE

SOMETHING HAD REALLY CHANGED.

Or was the problem that *nothing* had really changed?

Jenni McKay glanced out of the window at the view of inner-city Glasgow. A cityscape that was blurred by the rainwater streaming down the glass and dimmed by fading daylight. The grey sky was now several shades darker than the slate roofs of buildings that had been there for hundreds of years.

No changes there. In the buildings or the bad weather, but that was okay. Jenni loved this city and, unlike her brother who had taken jobs all over the world for the last ten years, she had no intention of going anywhere else for anything longer than a holiday. A place to call home had been what she'd always dreamed of every time she'd had her life packed up and moved somewhere new as a child.

The moaning sounds from the woman in the room with Jenni were as familiar as the view.

Sara was bouncing on a birth ball, leaning forward against the bed, and her partner, Callum, was rubbing her lower back. Sara reached for the mask attached to the Entonox cylinder and shoved it against her face, sucking in a deep breath. And then another, before dropping the mask again.

'I need to move,' she groaned.

'What would you like to do?' Jenni asked. 'Change your position or try walking around for a wee bit? Another shower?'

'I don't know,' Sara groaned. 'I'm so tired...'

'I know...' Jenni exchanged a sympathetic glance with Callum. The labour had started in the early hours of the morning and Sara had come into hospital as Jenni's shift had begun at seven a.m. They were all tired. 'How 'bout we get you back on the bed for a rest?'

'Yes, I think I'd like that... Are you going to check me again? I *must* be more than halfway dilated by now.'

On her back on the bed, Sara reached for the Entonox again as another contraction reached its peak. They were coming thick and fast now and Callum looked worried.

'Why are her legs shaking like that?' he asked.

'She's going into transition,' Jenni told him. She pulled off her gloves. 'Sara? You're fully dilated, love. You can start pushing with every contraction from now on.'

The rhythms and sounds and emotions of a normal labour were the same as ever. Jenni had long ago lost count of how many hundreds of babies she had delivered over her years as a midwife in a busy big city hospital. Each one was different. Some were dramatic, a few sadly tragic but, overall, each arrival of a new human into the world was an emotional journey for Jenni as well as the baby's family and she wouldn't want that to change in any way.

'Keep pushing, Sara…keep it going…more, more, more. I can see baby's head. Callum…as soon as this contraction ends, you can take Sara's hand and help her feel it…'

The look on Sara's face as she touched the dark, damp whorls of hair on her baby's head was one of complete awe and then determination, as her next contraction began.

'One more push, as *hard* as you can…'

The head emerged with almost a pop, face down. Jenni supported the head as it began to turn, lifting the body to help a shoulder free itself, and then the rest of the baby's body slid out into her hands. She lifted the slippery little person carefully, moving the baby girl onto her mother's chest. Sara looked completely stunned now— overwhelmed. She reached tentatively to touch her baby with both hands as Callum watched— tears rolling unchecked down his face and his camera on the bedside table completely forgotten.

Jenni rubbed the baby with a soft towel. She

hadn't made a sound yet but she was moving more and getting pinker. She wiped the face, considered reaching for a suction bulb, but then the little girl scrunched up her face with the effort of filling her lungs with enough air and opened her mouth to give her first cry—a wobbly warble that made Sara burst into tears herself.

'Oh…oh…it's okay, darling. You're here now. You're safe and…and we love you *so* much…'

Sara was cuddling the baby between her breasts now and Callum had one hand protectively covering their daughter's back and the other on Sara's head as he stroked the tangle of her hair. The expression on Sara's face as she looked up and lifted her face to meet his kiss took Jenni's breath away.

It also made her feel curiously…lonely…

And that was something she'd been aware of ever since she'd come back from her holiday in New Zealand and having time with her brother and her best friend. Back to living alone. Back to the frequent rain and greyness of Glasgow. Back to her work of helping other people achieve their dreams of families and futures.

That loneliness had been enough for her to do something that Grace had suggested during that visit and start the process of making an application to work as a midwife in New Zealand.

The motivation to go through the process was nothing more than an insurance policy, mind you. If she found herself missing her brother and her best friend too much, she could go back. For a longer, working, holiday. She would get homesick eventually and she would be only too glad to be here again and then she could finally settle, knowing that she was in the place she would always call home.

Jenni pulled a blanket over mother and baby to help keep them warm. She couldn't leave them alone in this private moment because she needed to do the APGAR scores on the baby and be there if anything unexpected happened to Sara like a post-partum haemorrhage, but she could step back enough for them to feel as if they were alone to welcome their daughter.

It would be time to clamp and cut the cord soon too, and then she could help Sara with her very first attempt to breast feed her baby—her favourite happy ending to her part in every birth.

She loved watching the baby react to the smell and touch of a mother's nipple and instinctively open their tiny mouth so wide and turn their head, ready to latch on. Sara would have her hand on the back of the head, waiting for that perfect moment to nudge it forward so that as much of the nipple as possible filled the baby's mouth before it closed and a primal instinct activated the muscles needed to suck.

And *that* was always the moment when emotion filled her like a tidal wave. When she could relax, knowing that her part in this everyday miracle was almost over and she could take a breath and simply enjoy the privilege of sharing such an intensely life-changing event for everyone involved. She'd had to blink back tears more often in recent times because the feeling had become noticeably more powerful.

Jenni knew it was the effect of her biological clock ticking more loudly as she got older, but it had never been quite like it was today. Her thirty-seventh birthday was only a few short months away and that was getting scarily close to turning forty, wasn't it?

Time was running out.

Maybe *this* was what had changed.

The familiar mix of relief and amazement expanded into the joy and palpable love in the room and exploded into a longing so intense that it felt like a vice closing over her ribcage and making it impossible to take a new breath.

She could hear an echo of her own voice in the back of her head.

'*...we made a vow that we were never going to get married or have kids...*'

She could see Dan's face as he'd listened to her saying that. She could even feel the tension that had been unleashed in the air around them—the current that was about to wash them into the most astonishing fantasy ever. The memory of which Jenni had found herself slipping back into almost every single night in the weeks since she'd arrived home. One that was never going to be tainted by reality because they were never going to see each other again so it was…perfect.

But it was also a fantasy that had absolutely no place in her head right now and had to be banished until she got home at the very least.

Was this another kind of fantasy that she should push aside? This longing to be holding her own baby like this? Skin to skin. With a tiny mouth smooshed onto her breast and the intimate sensation that sucking would create. What was it like, to know that you could give your precious newborn everything they needed to survive from your own body?

Jenni wasn't dismissing that vow completely, of course. She was never going to make the same mistakes her mother had, thinking that marriage—if only she could choose the right person—was the answer to living happily ever after. But she knew perfectly well that you didn't have to get married, or even have a long-term partner, to become a mother. She had been a midwife for many, many women who were facing parenthood alone for all sorts of reasons.

The longing that had stolen her breath so decisively morphed into something quite different. A realisation that this didn't have to be simply a fantasy. That it wasn't just feeding a baby that a mother could do entirely alone. It was a legitimate life choice these days, for a woman to have a baby and raise them alone. She didn't have to get married or have a committed partner. There were sperm banks where you got to choose the attributes you would want the father of your child to potentially provide. She'd gone online to find out more about them when she'd started having her first doubts, a year or more ago, about that vow to never have children, and had even signed up as a potential client in order to have access to more details about the donors, including their photographs, and what fishhooks might lie in wait down the track, like a child wanting information on their biological father or any half-siblings.

Jenni quietly retreated to let Callum and Sara have a few minutes alone as a brand-new family. She took the trolley with dirty linen and other used items into the sluice room. By the time she'd dealt with it all she could do a final check on Sara and her baby and it would be high time she headed home. She'd been on her feet for more than twelve hours now and she was very tired.

Maybe that was why it felt like something had changed. Why she was overreacting to seeing a newborn in her mother's arms and why the idea of going back to the sperm bank's website was refusing to get squashed. Perhaps the best way to deal with that would be to have another look?

Which was exactly what Jenni did when she ar-

rived home to the tiny, terraced house she'd managed to buy ten years ago—about the same time
that Jock had finished his training and early years
as a doctor and had chosen to use the small in-
heritance their mother had left them to start living
and working in countries increasingly far away
from Scotland. Having Grace live with her as a
flatmate had helped a lot with the mortgage but
Jenni was still coping financially and she wasn't
about to give up the security of owning her home,
especially if she was thinking about becoming a
single mother.

And she was, wasn't she?

Despite having decided long ago that she was
never going to get married or have children, Jenni's acceptance of single mothers had grown and
that unexpected desire to have a baby of her own
had taken root, to the extent that it seemed to be
finally overriding the long-held conviction that
letting history repeat itself and allowing a child
to grow up without a father in their life—as she
and Jock had done—was unacceptable because
it wasn't the 'perfect' family.

Somehow, she had persuaded herself that this
was completely different. Because *this* baby would
have a mother who wanted them. Who loved them
with all her heart. She and Jock hadn't known
who their father was, but they *had* known that
their mother hadn't wanted them because she'd
reminded them of that so frequently. That their

arrival had, in fact, apparently ruined her life so it wasn't any surprise that she didn't love them.

But Jenni would love her baby so much that it would make up for what she'd missed in her own life and the desire, after the delivery of Sara and Callum's baby, was strong enough for her to re-alise she was seriously considering the option of using a sperm donor.

Which was why she found herself curling up on her couch with a hot cup of tea and reading the donor profiles on the sperm bank website that ac-companied photos that caught her attention. She could find out the men's height, weight, ethnicity and even their skin tone and blood type.

She only skimmed the description of character-istics that told her someone was 'down-to-earth', 'patient and non-judgmental' or 'had the ability to always look on the bright side of life' because these were written by the men themselves. What was less likely to be biased were their educational qualifications and...hair colour.

Hair colour was important. Jenni needed to at least try and ensure her child didn't inherit the bright red hair that had meant she and Jock got mocked at school for being 'carrot-tops' or 'fire-crackers'. A dominant colour would be needed to counteract those genes. Black would be good.

Like Dan's hair...

Jenni scrolled through the images, discounting anyone who didn't have black hair.

Having a tertiary academic qualification was obviously a good indication of intelligence, so she filtered out occupations that only needed on-the-job training. Any kind of degree was acceptable but the ones with a medical connection were more attractive to Jenni. A vet, for example, or a physiotherapist or a doctor.

Like Dan...

With a sigh, Jenni closed her laptop. The fantasy of being a single mother at some point in the future was not nearly as compelling as letting herself drift back into the fantasy that Daniel Walker had provided in real life.

She could already feel that curl of desire, deep in her belly. She could see those sinfully dark eyes and feel the surprising softness of the waves of his hair. Memory was a wonderful thing when it could even conjure up the taste of a coffee martini flavoured kiss or the incredible heat of a tongue touching her own.

Oh...

This *had* to stop.

This fantasy might be delightful but it couldn't be allowed to influence her life going forward. How on earth was she going to be interested in ever dating anyone ever again if she let that one-night stand get entrenched as the bar for what sex should be like? It could ruin any further interactions she might have with men, which could end up being as disappointing as flying economy after being magically upgraded to first class for the first—and most likely *only*—time in one's life.

Jenni reached for her cup of tea, which would be cool enough to drink now. She took a sip but immediately screwed up her face.

'Yuck...'

It was undrinkable. The milk must have gone off.

Dan Walker moved out of the way to let his opponent try and hit the ball hard enough to bounce it off the front wall of the squash court, but Jock McKay missed the shot, which gave Dan the winning point for this game.

'Best of five?' Dan reached for his towel to mop his face in the ninety seconds' break they could have between games.

'Sure thing.' Jock picked up his water bottle. 'I'll win the next one.'

Dan grinned. 'Sure about that?'

'Aye.' Jock took another swallow of his water. 'I was distracted.'

Dan looked around the high, windowless walls of the small room they were in. 'Ah...of course you were.'

'I was thinking about a house Grace and I saw online today. Could be perfect for us. We're making a time to go and view it.'

'I guess that's the next step. Propose to a girl. Buy a house. Get married...'

'Whoa…you don't have to get married to buy a house and live together for ever, mate. And this place has got a jetty. Grace wants to know if that's the real attraction. She did suggest once that I just wanted to live happily ever after with my boat.'

'Sounds like a great idea to me.' Dan dropped his towel. He needed a mouthful of water too. Playing squash was physically demanding and he was out of shape. Jock seemed to have a lot less time for a session like this after work. Because he wanted to spend it with Grace?

Of course he did. They were head over heels in love with each other. Besotted, even…

Dan didn't want to think about what it would be like to be in that space. He picked up his racquet.

'Ready?'

'Almost.' Jock was checking his phone. And shaking his head. 'It's raining in Glasgow,' he said. 'Who knew…?'

Dan couldn't help himself, even though he knew it wasn't the best idea to let his lips form her name. 'Message from Jenni?'

'Aye…'

'How is she?'

'Okay, I think. Took her a while to get used to being back home after her trip. She loved it here. Loved Melbourne too.'

'She was visiting a friend there, wasn't she?'

Jock nodded as he swapped his phone for his racquet. 'An old boyfriend, it was. Her first, in fact. They haven't seen each other for about twenty years.'

Dan made a sound that was no more than a grunt. Almost a growl…

Good grief…was he *jealous* of an old boyfriend of a woman he was probably never going to see again?

No. This was relief, that was what it was. It would make it even easier to not be distracted by any thoughts of women, unlike Jock.

Dan picked up the ball they needed. 'My serve, I believe.'

It was. Because he'd won the last game. He might be winning every squash game with Jock for quite some time, given that he would never be in any danger of being distracted in that way himself.

He'd needed that reminder of how disruptive it could be. Because, if he was honest, he *had* found himself thinking, rather too much, about the night he'd had with Jock's sister.

Oh…*man*…

That sensation of pure…what was it? Lust? Desire? *Need…?*

Whatever it was, it was powerful enough to instantly cut through the physical—and mental—focus needed to see where that tiny rubber ball was heading at warp speed and intercept it to get it back to the front wall.

It was only there for a nanosecond. A flash

sparked by the memory of the best sex he'd ever had in his life. He could almost feel his fingers buried in those waves of hair the colour of flames as he'd cradled her head to try and savour just one more kiss…

He could hear the music of the accent in her voice and smell the scent of her skin.

He could see those extraordinarily blue eyes. A gaze that held his as if there was no space between them at all and…it felt like a connection he'd never known existed. It almost felt as familiar as looking into a mirror, but this was with a perfect stranger and that made it…weird.

Dangerous, even.

Thank goodness Jenni had left the country the very next day and was now safely back home on the other side of the world.

The flash of the memory with its inherent urgent warning was over in virtually the same blink of time with which he'd registered its presence.

But it had been long enough to be disturbing.

And long enough to miss an easy shot. The first point of this game was Jock's so it was no surprise that he could see a triumphant grin in his peripheral vision.

His opponent's confidence was premature, however.

Dan knew exactly how to conquer a distraction like that.

It wasn't going to happen again.

* * *

Life was full of ironies, Jenni thought as she stared at the small window in the middle of the plastic stick she was holding.

She was a midwife. She should have recognised the signs of pregnancy long before this.

She'd been scrolling through potential candidates on a sperm donor site, for heaven's sake, when she'd been pregnant already.

She'd told herself the milk was off. That her periods were irregular anyway so it was no surprise that international travel had made them even less reliable.

So here she was, not only pregnant but probably a couple of months along.

Okay…who was she kidding? Jenni knew the *exact* date of this conception. Which meant she knew exactly who the father of this baby was.

Daniel Walker.

Her brother's best friend.

And there was another irony. She'd warned her brother not to even think about hitting on *her* best friend when Grace had decided to go and work in New Zealand, because she'd been worried that somebody would get hurt and relationships between both siblings and friends could be damaged.

Now Jock and Grace were madly in love. *Engaged* even, and had just purchased a property together.

Dan had not only made his feelings about significant relationships known but he also clearly believed he was incapable of fathering a child. How was Dan going to react when he learned that he was mistaken? How was *Jock* going to react when he discovered just how his friend had looked after his sister when they'd been left alone together on the first night they'd met?

Would the bomb that Jenni was inevitably going to have to drop be enough to destroy a friendship and make things weird between herself and her brother?

The urge to talk this through with her best friend was strong enough to make Jenni reach for her phone, but she didn't make the call. She couldn't tell Grace because she couldn't ask her to keep a secret from the person she loved enough to be planning to spend the rest of her life with him. And what if Dan had said anything to Jock about what had happened that night they'd been left alone together? It wasn't rocket science to put two and two together and guess who the father was. Letting someone else reveal this news was dodging a responsibility that was entirely her own.

Jenni didn't have to tell anybody anything just yet, though, did she? Things could go wrong in a first trimester.

And maybe she didn't want to tell anybody until she had got her own head around this. She could keep this a secret at least until she didn't feel quite so stunned.

It took another week before the shock began to wear off properly but, when it did, Jenni could feel the tendrils of quite another reaction beginning to grow. When another week passed and she saw the images on her first ultrasound examination, she knew that this was meant to be.

This was Fate giving her the gift of something she'd wanted for even longer than she had admitted to herself. Being a mother. Being able to protect and love and *want* a child. To give him, or her, the life that she wished she and Jock had been given.

No…to give *them* that life she and her brother should have had.

Was Fate pleased with herself, repeating history by doubling up on this miracle? The genetic likelihood of conceiving fraternal twins *was* hereditary, but Jenni hadn't even considered the possibility so she found she had tears rolling down her face when the ultrasound technician turned the screen and she could see the distinct shape of two babies in her womb.

This twist in just how much her life was going to change made it more complicated to figure out how to drop the bombshell news. It wasn't something to put in an email. Or a video call. Especially knowing just how shocked Dan was going to be. It didn't matter that Jenni intended to be a single parent so she wasn't expecting—and might not even welcome—any major input from the father of these babies, there was no getting away from the fact that he had the right to be a part of their lives if he chose to be.

And part of Jenni really wanted him to make that choice, because that was something else she and Jock had wished for when they were growing up without even knowing who their father was. They would be living on opposite sides of the world but that didn't necessarily mean that he couldn't be as important to his children as Jock and Grace would be. Technology made sharing lives so much easier now and Jenni loved what she'd seen of New Zealand so far. If she could afford it, she wouldn't be opposed to an annual holiday in the country that represented half the heritage of these babies.

This was going to be life-changing news for Dan. And for Jock, who was going to become an uncle. An uncle of *twins*. Jock and Jenni both knew how special that bond was.

It was news that needed to be delivered face to face, Jenni decided. But how would she explain why she was planning another visit so soon after the last when it was such a long journey and so expensive?

There was too much to think about in the next few days and while Jenni was finding it progressively easier to imagine herself as a mother, the prospect of revealing her news was daunting enough to make it preferable to put off making any decisions.

A wake-up call came with an email that arrived unexpectedly in her inbox from the New Zealand Midwifery Council to say that her application for registration had been successful. There would still be interviews and assessments to be ticked off in person but, with a work visa already added to her passport, Jenni could theoretically start looking for a job as a midwife in New Zealand. She had no intention of actually doing that, but it could be a legitimate reason for another visit to the country.

And then an even better one presented itself. Where she would be able to dodge any questions and guilt that she could be seen as deceiving the people she cared most about because she wouldn't have to tell anybody she was coming.

It could be a surprise visit. And what better reason for a surprise visit than a birthday? Jenni would be well into her second trimester by the date of her shared birthday with Jock and it might be hard to keep her secret that long, but perhaps Fate was giving her this time as well. So that she could plan and dream about the future before having to face the shock—and understandable concern—from everybody else involved. And what if Dan turned his back on acknowledging his children? Was she ready to deal with a rejection that could open old wounds for both herself and Jock?

When Jenni opened a calendar to choose a date that was early enough to allow for the international travel and time zone changes and let her arrive on the right day, she saw the note that Jock and Grace were planning to move into their new house the following week so they'd be in the middle of getting packed up, wouldn't they?

Should she change her travel plans?

No. Jenni drew a big circle around the date she'd chosen.

Having the distraction of moving might be the perfect way to demonstrate that her news wasn't going to stop the world turning and life could continue as normal. And what better time to reveal the impending birth of *her* babies than the day to celebrate the birth of their mother and uncle? With a new auntie and…maybe even Dan if he wanted to be involved in their lives in an acceptable way.

He was their father, after all.

Part of their family.

And he had the right to be part of their lives.

CHAPTER TWO

'*SURPRISE!* HAPPY BIRTHDAY, JOCK.'

Jenni put down her suitcase so that she could hug her brother with one arm.

Jock hugged her back. 'And to you… But…' He was still blinking at her in astonishment. 'You haven't come all the way across the world to celebrate our birthday, have you?'

'Why not?' Jenni tried to sound offhand. If the oversized top she was wearing wasn't doing a good enough job of hiding the newly discernible bump of her pregnancy, the bunch of balloons and carry bag she had in her other hand were an additional disguise.

'Well, it's rather a long way to come when I hadn't even planned any kind of a party,' Jock said. He waved a hand at a stack of boxes in the hallway by the front door. 'We're in a bit of a mess, what with packing and all the chaos that goes with moving house.'

'We can make our own party. I've got cake. And wine. Or we can go out to dinner.'

'Am I missing something?' Jock sounded distinctly puzzled. 'We've never made that big a deal out of our birthdays and it's not a milestone like turning forty or something.' He took Jenni's suitcase and turned to lead her into the house. 'Not that Dan celebrated when *he* turned forty recently, but he's not really a party kind of guy, I guess…'

Jenni needed to take a big breath.

Hearing Dan's name being spoken aloud suddenly made this very real. She was here. She would be seeing Dan very soon.

And she was feeling very nervous…

Jock had to be picking up on that nervousness because his tone suggested that he was sensing an undercurrent that was disturbing him. Had she made a huge mistake keeping this secret for so long? Not in giving herself time to get used to this before bringing Dan into the picture, but what if Jock and Grace were going to be angry at being excluded for so long? Or worse, hurt by having such a life-changing secret being hidden?

She opened her mouth to try and give Jock a heads-up that she did have another important reason for being here, but she couldn't think of how to broach the subject. Maybe she needed Grace here to potentially dilute the impact just a little. Or maybe she had become too good at procrastinating.

'Can I have the same room I had last time I was

here?' she asked brightly instead. 'You don't have a houseful of new hospital employees, do you?'

'Yes. And no. And you do realise we're about to move into the house we've bought, don't you? Our settlement date is next week.'

'I know. Grace told me. And I've seen pictures of the house, which is absolutely gorgeous…'

Just the mention of Grace's name was enough to change Jock's characteristically cheeky grin into the soppiest smile she had ever seen on his face. This was a man who was utterly in love and while they chatted about the house as they made their way to the kitchen, Jenni had to blink back the mistiness of knowing how happy her brother was.

'Where *is* Grace?' she asked eventually.

'Out on a home visit. Do you remember the last night you were here on your visit? When we had to abandon you to go and see the woman who'd been in a car accident?'

'And you left me with Dan?' Jenni laughed but it sounded forced, even to her own ears. 'Yes, I do remember.'

The tension was escalating. She *had* to reveal her secret. Soon…

She could barely focus on what Jock was telling her about the happy aftermath of the woman from the accident that night giving birth to a healthy baby not long ago.

At least some of that tension dissipated when

the wait for Grace to arrive home ended and she walked into the kitchen with an expression of complete disbelief on her face.

'*Jenni*...what on earth are *you* doing here?'

'*Surprise...*' Jenni held out her arms and Grace met her halfway across the kitchen floor.

'It's our birthday,' Jock said. 'Apparently, Jenni decided she needed to come and celebrate.'

Oh...the look of love that passed between Jock and Grace excluded Jenni completely for a moment and she got a flashback to that odd loneliness she'd been haunted by after her return to Glasgow. She thought that had been buried the moment she knew that she was on the way to creating her own little family, but it caught her by surprise again now as she watched her brother and her best friend share a very tender kiss and it was sharp enough for her to make a sound of discomfort.

'I am *here*, you know.'

There was laughter in the room as well as all that love. A short time later, Jock was taking the bottle of champagne Jenni had brought with her from the fridge and Grace was finding glasses.

'Not for me,' Jenni said as Grace took a third champagne flute from the cupboard.

Three tiny words but they fell into the room with the effect of a match lighting a grenade fuse. The pop of the cork shooting out of the bottle Jock was holding added a rather appropriate explosion into the sudden silence.

Jenni could almost feel the pennies dropping around her. They both knew how much she loved champagne. They both believed she was here, at least in part, to celebrate a birthday.

'Aye…' She tried, and failed, to defuse the atmosphere with a smile. 'I'm pregnant.'

They were still staring at her. 'How far along?' Grace breathed.

'About seventeen weeks.'

Jock was an obstetrician. Grace was a midwife. In the time it took for them to share a glance with each other, they'd done the calculations and come up with an approximate conception date.

'It happened on your holiday?'

'Yes.'

Grace's eyes widened. 'Was it Melbourne? You and…what was his name—your first ever boyfriend? Jeremy?'

'No…' Jenni was shocked. 'We had lunch. He showed me around Melbourne. Jeremy's *married.* I met his wife and kids.' She shook her head, appalled that either of them would think that was even a possibility.

'It couldn't have been anyone here.' Jock was frowning as he thought aloud. 'You were with one of us the whole time you were in New Zealand.'

But Grace caught his gaze again. 'Not the *whole* time,' she murmured. 'We left her alone with Dan, remember? When we got called back into work.'

Jock looked as if something might be hurting him physically. 'But he said he was going to look after Jenni.'

He swallowed visibly. 'I don't believe this…'

He looked down at the bottle of champagne he was still holding. 'When I told Dan it was my birthday he said he might drop in later to have a beer. Does he know *you're* here?'

He looked up. He *was* hurt. Jenni's heart broke a little.

She shook her head. 'I decided I needed to tell him in person. I needed to be sure of how I felt about it myself and…and I wanted to wait until I was in my second trimester just in case…' She could feel tears prickling at the back of her eyes. 'And then I thought you'd guess something was up if told you I was coming back so soon and it wasn't that much longer to wait to have the excuse of coming for our birthday.' The tears were starting to spill. 'I'm sorry I didn't tell you sooner.'

'Oh… *Jenni…*'

Grace's arms were around her, but Jenni pulled back. 'There's more,' she confessed. 'It's *twins…*'

Somehow, that changed everything. This was history threatening to repeat itself and she could see Jock being dragged back in time. Remembering their childhood. The times when it felt like they only had each other in a world where no one really wanted them. Where they only had one parent—the one who hadn't been able to walk away so easily?

'I don't want my babies growing up not knowing who their father is,' Jenni said quietly. 'Like we did. Or that there's a man out there somewhere who has no idea that he is a father. What if our father had known we existed, Jock? Maybe he would have come to find us. He might have *wanted* us and…and everything would have been so different…'

It was Jock who was folding her into his arms now. 'Do you want us here when you tell Dan?'

Jenni shook her head again. 'Best I do that by myself, I think.' She made a huff of sound that was almost laughter. 'Would you believe we spent most of that night talking about how much we liked being single? I told him about our vow to never get married or have kids. He told me he *couldn't* have kids…' She let her next breath out as a sigh. 'I have a feeling he might not be too happy about getting this news.'

The last thing Dan expected when he arrived at the old villa, to see if his mate wanted that beer he'd promised, was to find Jock's sister sitting on the top of the steps that led to the veranda.

No…the *very* last thing he expected was the rush of feeling that followed the shock of recognising that it was Jenni McKay. It was, weirdly, almost relief. He couldn't deny that he'd thought about her so often he had missed her presence as almost a physical ache sometimes. Or maybe it was joy rather than relief. He'd thought he might never see Jenni again but here she was—as if someone had waved a magic wand and made his wish come true.

'Hey…' He could feel his smile stretching muscles that hadn't been used that much lately. 'When did you arrive?'

'Today.' Jenni was smiling back at him. 'Just a couple of hours ago.'

Her gaze was holding his and Dan got the impression that she was just as surprised by how she was feeling about seeing *him* again. Or was he simply seeing a reflection of how he was feeling? How *happy* he was suddenly feeling…

'And you're still awake? I'm impressed.'

'I'll crash soon. After the birthday party.'

'That's why I'm here. To wish Jock a happy birthday.'

'He'll be back soon. He and Grace have gone to the supermarket to get some more boxes for packing. And they're going to pick up Thai takeaways or fish and chips on the way home.'

There was no point going inside by himself and he'd be able to see Jock returning home from here—hopefully soon. Dan put down the chilled six-pack of lager he was carrying and sank onto the step beside Jenni.

'Fancy a beer?'

'No, thank you.'

'It didn't occur to me to pick up anything as exotic as a black margarita, sorry.'

Oh, *help*... Why on earth had he said that? It would have been far more sensible to avoid any reminders of that night. Just the mention of her choice of drink and he caught a flash of how it had felt being with her in that cocktail bar. Watching the way her face lit up as she smiled. Feeling the first spikes of a physical attraction that was... almost illicit, after promising Jock he would take care of his sister. Unwise, anyway, but that only gave it an edge he'd never had the pleasure of experiencing before.

Dan blew out a careful breath. Was Jenni remembering that evening as well? He needed to steer them back onto safe territory. Fast.

'So that's why you're here? For Jock's birthday?'

'It's my birthday too.'

'Of course it is. Sorry... I forgot about that twin thing.' He found a smile. 'Happy birthday, Jenni.'

'Thanks. I hear you had a big one recently.'

Dan shrugged. 'Age is just a number. I don't do birthday parties.' He gave Jenni a quizzical glance. 'I didn't think Jock did either.'

'Neither of us do. We were lucky anyone remembered when we were kids.'

'But you've come this far to celebrate this birthday?'

'That's one of the reasons I came, yes...' Jenni's gaze slid away from his.

A faint sensation, like a chill, ran down Dan's spine.

They both sat in silence for a long moment, staring down the street as if they were both hoping that the distraction of Jock and Grace returning would be available.

It wasn't. And Dan suddenly had a thought that might explain that odd premonition.

'You're not planning to come and live here, are you?' he asked.

'What on earth makes you say *that*?'

Her glance was startled. More than startled. It looked like a flight or fight response had just been triggered. Jenni looked...*frightened*...?

'It was something Jock said a while back. That he never wanted to move back to Scotland but that he and Grace were working on a plan to persuade you to come and live in New Zealand.'

Jenni shook her head sharply. 'Scotland is my home,' she said. 'I have no intention of living anywhere else.'

Dan could feel a wash of something like relief now. Because he'd never factored in *seeing* Jenni McKay again, let alone living in the same town. He only ever indulged in sexual encounters when there was no likelihood of that happening.

Or at least no chance of being unable to escape being in close proximity unexpectedly. The sort of occasions that might occur if they had mutual friends, perhaps—or having to work together. He'd learned long ago that the ideal scenario was when he was on holiday a long way from home. Or with someone who was on holiday here and just passing through, like Jenni had been. He'd already spent far too much time thinking about that night he'd had with her.

Dreaming about it.

Coming to terms with the fact that he was probably never, ever going to experience sex like that again in his lifetime.

Oh, man…he could actually feel the pull of this woman again right now, as he sat this close to her. By some trick of the mind, he could sense the warmth and scent of her skin. He could even imagine that he could *taste* her, and in that instant he knew he was in trouble.

That pull was irresistible. If he even made eye contact with Jenni while this spear of desire was simultaneously touching every cell in his body, he could imagine it would be contagious enough to have them kissing passionately within a heartbeat and it was a no-brainer what would happen next…

So he stared down the street again. And then he cleared his throat as if that might stem that disturbing level of physical attraction he was experiencing.

'I also wanted to see you,' Jenni said into this new, slightly awkward silence.

'Oh...?' Dan risked the eye contact. Because... if Jenni was only here for a holiday again, didn't that make it just bending the rules about his sex life a little and not breaking them enough to be a problem?

'I'm pregnant, Dan...'

The words didn't make any sense. Oh, he could understand them, of course, but why was she telling *him*? He could feel himself frowning and raising his eyebrows at the same time, which made his whole face feel strangely tight.

'Ah...congratulations?' Should he say anything else? 'Are you...happy about that?'

'Yes.' The affirmation had a thoughtful tone but it was surprisingly decisive.

'Does Jock know?'

'Yes.' He could hear Jenni taking a deeper breath. 'But I had to tell you too. That's the main reason I'm here.'

That chill was back again. This time it had sharp edges—like claws. 'I don't understand...'

'You were wrong, Dan,' Jenni said quietly. 'About never being able to have kids. I'm not here to mess with your life or ask for any kind of commitment, but you have the right to know that you're going to be a father.'

It looked like an almost automatic gesture to put both her hands on her belly, smoothing out that floppy top. Dan could see the soft mound of what he could very easily remember as being a delicious area of skin between Jenni's hipbones that had been as flat as a pancake when he'd put his own hands there not that long ago.

Her words became muffled by a noise that was rather like the static that came from not being quite on an exact radio frequency. There was interference as well, that came in the form of long-buried memories suddenly escaping their prison.

'I'm pregnant, Dan.'

'No way...it's not possible.'

'It's happened. See?' His wife had held up the test stick for him to see the lines in the window.

'But they said I had far more chance of winning the lottery than getting you pregnant.'

'Are you happy?'

'I'm stunned. And...yes, of course I'm happy. Beyond happy. It's what we wanted. It's everything I've ever wanted. A family of my own...'

Dan ruthlessly slammed the door shut on the ghost of that conversation before any more of his ex-wife's words reappeared. Getting to his feet seemed to have helped, although he had no memory of having moved. That lack of control over his body seemed to apply to what he was saying as well.

'You don't expect me to *believe* that, do you?'

Jenni wasn't saying anything. She had wrapped her arms around her knees and her head was bent.

'You *do* remember that I told you I was infertile?'

'That's part of the reason I thought you should know.' Jenni's voice was quiet. Expressionless. 'Just in case, you know…you got carried away with someone else and thought there was no reason to worry about not having any protection available.' She wasn't looking up at him. 'And yes, I know you can have a very low sperm count after a bad dose of mumps, but it only takes one that gets to the right place at the right time.'

'Not going to happen when that "one" probably has motility and morphology issues that render it completely useless.' Dan could hear the ice in his voice. 'Why are you doing this, Jenni? Why aren't you sitting on the step of that old boyfriend of yours that you went to see in Melbourne on your way home from here?'

Or had it been before then? Had she already been pregnant when she'd come here on holiday?

He'd seen the obvious weight gain on her belly when she'd outlined it with her hands. A quick mental calculation told him it was less than four months since their night together. It wasn't normal to have that much of a bump this early in a pregnancy, was it?

'How did you know that?'

'Jock told me. He got a text message from you when we were playing a game of squash not long after you'd gone home. I asked how you were and

he said you'd loved your visit to Melbourne and
that you'd had a good time catching up with someone you hadn't seen for twenty years. I've heard
that you never forget your first...'

Jenni had gone very pale. He could see individual freckles dotted over the bridge of her nose and
the top of her cheekbones as she finally looked
up at him. She looked so shocked that Dan could
feel a cloud of misgiving forming around him.

He ignored it. He was just as shocked that she
would be suggesting this in the first place. 'You
want me to do a DNA test to prove that I'm not
the father of your baby, Jenni? Fine...bring it on.'

She still didn't say anything. And Dan finally
realised that he'd probably said too much.

He didn't bother picking up the cans of lager
he'd brought to share with Jock. He couldn't wait
a second longer to get away from this.

From those ghosts.

From Jenni...

'Was that Dan's car I saw going past us when we
came out of the chip shop?'

'Could well have been...' Jenni was still sitting
on the step. 'He couldn't get away fast enough
after I told him I was pregnant.'

'It will have been a massive shock,' Grace said.
'I imagine he's going to need some time to get
used to the idea.'

'He's not going to get used to it.' Jenni shrugged.

'He doesn't believe it. He made it very clear that he thinks the real father is Jeremy. That I'm… I'm deliberately *lying* to him.'

The tears Jenni had been holding back were way too close to the surface now, but there was more than disappointment causing her distress. It was beginning to feel more like…*anger*…

Jock and Grace exchanged a glance that seemed to be a whole conversation.

'I'm going to put the kettle on,' Grace said. 'And make some tea. I'll be back soon.'

She was leaving Jenni alone with Jock, wasn't she? And it was the best thing she could have done. Because Jock understood.

'I told him, that night,' Jenni said as Jock sat where Dan had been sitting only minutes before. 'I said that I can't abide lies. That I'd *never* tell them myself. You know what *he* said?'

Of course he didn't. Jock hadn't been there. If he had been, Jenni wouldn't be here now.

'He said "How do I know *that's* not a lie?" And I just smiled and said that it didn't matter because we were never going to see each other again.'

That was enough to flick the switch. Jenni burst into tears. 'It's going to be us all over again, Jock. Two little kids who are never going to have a daddy or feel like they have a real home.'

Jock put his arm over Jenni's shoulders. 'It's not going to be anything like us,' he said quietly.

'I promise. And *you* know I never make promises I can't keep.'

Jenni did know that. It was for the same reason she never lied. A broken promise was just another kind of lie, and they both knew the disappointment—despair, even—that the aftermath could bring, especially to children who had yet to learn not to hope that this time really would be different.

'Of course I'll be there to pick you up after school...'

'Yes... Father Christmas is coming this year. He won't forget again...'

'It'll be different this time. I promise... We'll be a real family...'

Jock's quiet voice dispersed the ghosts from their childhood.

'These babies are going to have a mum who's never going to let them think that she never wanted them or that they've ruined her life,' he said. 'They're going to have an uncle and auntie who will love them to bits and never break any promises. You don't need Daniel Walker in your life.'

'I know... I didn't even *want* him in my life.' Jennie sniffed hard and rubbed her nose on her sleeve. 'He told me to do a DNA test so he could prove he wasn't the father, but you know what?'

'What?'

'I'm not going to. Not before they're born, anyway. If he actually believes I'd lie about something this important, he's not someone I want in my life. I'll do it later, when I'm back on the other side of the world and these babies are safely born, but as far as I'm concerned he's just thrown away his right to know for sure that he's going to be a father and to share in this pregnancy and the birth of his children.'

'So you told him it was twins?'

Jenni's huff of laughter was anything but amused. 'Are you kidding? When he reacted like that to the idea of one baby, there was no way I was going to double up on the bad news.'

Jock squeezed her shoulders tighter for a moment. 'I'm sorry, Jen. Can't say I'm overly impressed with Dan right now.'

'Neither am I.' Grace was back with a tray that had a teapot and mugs on it. She set it down on the wrought-iron table between two chairs on the veranda. 'But I'd like to know why he's so sure he can't have kids.'

'Bad dose of mumps when he was young, apparently,' Jenni said.

'Only takes one good swimmer to do the deed,' Jock murmured. 'I've seen more than one surprise pregnancy from a dad who had a low sperm count.'

'That's what I told him,' Jenni said. 'But he just muttered something about the motility and morphology being useless.'

'That kind of makes sense.' Jock gave Jenni another squeeze and then let her go so that she could reach up to take the mug of tea Grace was offering. 'Even the success of invasive procedures like intracytoplasmic sperm injections and IVF relies on those factors. Sounds like he's been properly tested. Not that it's something I've ever talked to him about.'

'And it's not something I intend to talk to him about again,' Jenni said. 'I'm sorry, Jock. I've kind of ruined our birthday, haven't I?'

'We're not going to let it,' Jock told her. He snapped his fingers. 'I know…we're going to celebrate on UK time, which means that it will still be our birthday tomorrow. I've got an afternoon off. What are you doing, Grace?'

'I've got a home visit booked in, but it's more of a social one because it's well outside the official six-weeks' follow-up for new mums. The department's been given a sample of a new breastfeeding wraparound pillow for using with twins and I was going to take a water taxi and deliver it to Tessa so that she can try it out and give us some feedback. You remember me telling you about the twins we delivered when that cyclone hit while you were on your way back to Scotland, Jen?'

She nodded. 'I was asking Jock about them just before you got home today. He said that was when he proposed to you.'

'It was…' Grace and Jock shared a glance that

looked as though it was about to turn into a kiss, but then Jock broke the eye contact.

'I've just had the best idea. Why don't Jenni and I take you over to visit Tessa? We might get lucky and see some dolphins.'

'Oh, no…' Jenni widened her eyes theatrically. 'You think I'm going to get on your boat? So you can push me off again like you did when we were kids?'

Jock was grinning at her. 'You fell off that boat,' he said. 'You were leaning over the side too far because you thought you could see a fish. I was trying to *catch* you.'

Jenni had always known that was true. She also knew that she hadn't been in any real danger in the knee-deep pond, but she'd never quite forgiven her brother for laughing at her instead of being the hero who had always been there to protect or comfort her. He was stepping up now though, wasn't he? He wanted to be here for her in a new phase in her life that was rather more serious than getting wet and muddy by falling out of a boat.

And she needed him as much as she had when she had been bullied at school, yet again, for being the new girl. Or for being one of those twins whose mother couldn't be bothered looking after them properly.

No…right now she needed him more than she ever had before.

CHAPTER THREE

IT TURNED OUT that Jock's idea to take Jenni out on his boat the next afternoon had been inspired.

It was exactly what the doctor ordered to break the remarkably unpleasant quicksand of emotions like anger and confusion, disappointment and anxiety. There were shades of betrayal that were lurking as well, after Jock and Grace had considered, however briefly, the possibility that she might have slept with Jeremy, and having someone believe that she was deliberately lying about something *this* important had delivered a blow that felt as visceral as a physical attack.

The exhaustion of jetlag fortunately meant that her misery didn't stop Jenni falling deeply asleep, but it coloured her dreams as she slept the clock around and then lingered to make her feet feel leaden when she woke to find she was alone in the house because Jock and Grace had already left for work. Those emotions had become even more intense as she sat outside and relived Dan's visit last night.

Unbelievably, there was another element trying to edge its way into the anger she felt towards him.

That curl of sensation she'd experienced when she first saw him again after so many weeks, walking towards her. How *happy* she'd been to see him. Just as tall. Just as dark and, if anything, even more attractive, because she could remember—all too well in way too intimate detail—just how amazing it had been to have this man make love to her.

Okay, so it wasn't really a *curl* of sensation, like something gentle and pleasant. No…it was more like a spear with a sharp point that caused pain as it scythed a path through the core of her body.

Sheer physical desire, that was what it was…

Unwanted.

Unacceptable. Especially now that he'd deemed her dishonest. Deceitful. Someone who wasn't worth knowing.

Could his reaction be excused by the fact that he'd had a shock? That he had genuinely believed that he wasn't capable of fathering a child?

Yes.

No…

Okay…*yes*…but Jenni wasn't ready to accept that. Perhaps because part of her wanted an excuse to pat herself on the back for having done the right thing and then disappear back into her own life, where she would have no interference in how she raised her family.

Even a walk through the pretty township of Picton hadn't really helped her internal arguments and low mood, but watching the uncoiling of the ropes that tethered Jock's lovely clinker-built cabin cruiser boat named *Lassie* to the bollards on the pier made it feel as if some of those horrible knots in Jenni's gut were also unravelling. Gliding smoothly through the still waters of the marina towards the more open sea of the Sounds increased that relief by several notches. They were leaving the town behind.

She was leaving Dan behind, along with the whole tangle of the bond that had inadvertently been created between them.

How much better was it going to be to get on a plane and feel that distance becoming the solid barrier of thousands of miles?

No…best not to try and imagine that. Because Jenni had the sneaking suspicion that it might not be better at all and that she might be leaving behind more than she wanted to, even when she took Jock and Grace out of the equation.

The peacefulness of this stunning scenery was soothing as they motored towards the humps and peaks of forest-covered peninsulas and islands emerging from deep, clear blue water.

Jenni and Grace were sitting on either side of *Lassie*'s deck. Jock was under the canopy at the wheel but with the engine running at a gentle speed and the silence around them being broken only by the occasional cry of a seagull, it was easy to hear him when he looked over his shoulder to speak.

'Grace and I were talking about you on the way home this afternoon,' he said.

Jenni found a smile. 'I can't imagine why.' Her smile faded. 'Did you see Dan at work?'

'No.' Jock's tone was tight. 'Which is probably just as well. I'm too angry to want to talk to him right now.' He turned back to watch where he was steering the boat.

'I'm sorry, Jock...' Jenni's breath came out in a heartfelt sigh. 'Please don't let this wreck a friendship for you. Friends are important.'

'Not as important as a sister.' He turned again to throw her a smile. 'Which was what Grace and I were actually talking about. It's going to be okay, Jen.'

'It *is*,' Grace said.

Jenni swallowed hard. 'I know...'

'We're going to do whatever we can to help,' Grace added.

'We thought you might like to think about coming to live here,' Jock said. 'So we could really help with the babies, especially in the early days.'

'I can't do that.' Jenni shook her head. 'Glasgow's home. And home is as important as friends. I've got some of those there as well, you know. They'll help. And I love my wee house. I wouldn't have anywhere to live here.'

'You could live with us,' Jock said. 'We're your family.'

'You could both come and live in Scotland,' Jenni countered. 'That's your real home. And you've still got family in England, Grace, so it's close to home for you too.'

This time, when Jock turned back, it was Grace he was looking at and they shared a long glance. And a smile.

'Look around you,' Grace said. 'Why would anyone want to live anywhere else?'

Silence fell between them as Jenni did what she was told and gazed out at the scenery again.

'This is the Queen Charlotte Sound,' Jock told her a short time later. 'Which is the main drag for marine traffic into Picton. We're heading for Kumutoto Bay, which only has access by boat.'

'That would have been a challenge when Tessa was expecting twins.'

'Nobody expected a cyclone,' Grace put in. 'But yeah…there's always a risk that twins are going to arrive early.' She was holding Jenni's gaze. 'I'll be worried about you,' she added quietly. 'If you're too far away.'

'It's going to be okay…' Jenni liked the sound of her new mantra. 'You'll see.'

The water became an astonishing shade of almost emerald-green in the shallows of Kumutoto

Bay and both Jock and Jenni were invited into the house for Grace's visit to Tessa and her twins. Watching this new mother handle both her babies as she tried out the new type of breastfeeding support pillow was a very welcome bonus to this outing.

Jenni felt better than she had in a long time as they motored back to the marina in Picton. Maybe since she'd acquired a very new level of anxiety after seeing those two lines in the window of that pregnancy test.

'I can't believe how easy Tessa made it look to be looking after twins on her own.'

'She's not on her own. She's got a very supportive husband.'

'She was on her own this afternoon. And she was coping just fine.' Jenni's smile was confident. 'I'm going to be like Tessa. Just minus the husband bit. Because, you know, I did make a vow that I was never going to get married.'

Jock laughed. 'That vow was about never having kids either. You're breaking that part.'

'So are you. You're engaged to be married.'

'Only to one person. You're *double* breaking the part about the kids.'

They were all laughing by now and the smile stayed with Jenni as Jock slowed *Lassie* to enter the marina.

She didn't need to upend her entire life and move to a new country.

And she didn't need Dan Walker...

That smile vanished a short time later, however, when *Lassie* bumped gently into the pier as the ripple of a swell from an outgoing boat made her rock.

'Can you get the rope, please, Grace? And throw it around the bollard?'

'Sure.'

Grace climbed up on the seat with the coil of rope in her hands. She went to step onto the pier to get close enough to the bollard just as another ripple reached *Lassie*. Jock was busy trying to keep the boat steady against the wooden pier so it was only Jenni who saw Grace's foot slip. She fell onto the pier rather than into the water, which was a good thing, but her foot ended up between the side of the boat and the wooden pole on the pier as she fell, and that was most definitely *not* a good thing. Jenni thought she could actually hear the crack of a breaking bone.

Jock certainly heard Grace cry out in pain. He cut the engine and leapt from the back of the boat to the pier. He took the rope and hastily secured *Lassie* but it was Grace he was focused on as she was dragging herself further away from the edge of the pier. It didn't need medical training in order to see how bad this was. Grace's foot was at a very odd angle to her leg. It was clearly a nasty dislocation and probable fracture of her ankle.

She was as white as a ghost and Jock didn't look much better as he took his phone out.

'Don't move,' he told Grace. 'I'm calling an ambulance…'

Well…this was awkward.

Responding to a call to the emergency department, Daniel Walker found himself face to face with Jock McKay as he approached the central desk. He hadn't been this close to Jock since he'd told him he might drop in to share a birthday beer with him yesterday.

Before his sister had told him that she was pregnant.

And that he was the father of the baby.

He'd been so angry when he'd walked out on Jenni to go home. He had, in fact, changed his clothes the minute he was through the door and had gone for a very long run. Long enough to begin to succeed in burning off the anger that had scorched its way through the shock. Anger that he couldn't control this shove back into a past he'd worked so hard to get over. Anger that he had to feel the pain of his whole life imploding all over again. Burying it for so many years had, strangely, not reduced its power to hurt. If anything, that surprise ambush had made it even sharper.

Because it was history repeating itself.

And he hadn't been able to shut out the extra echoes of his ex-wife's voice after all. Those casual words that had destroyed his dreams—and his life as he'd known it then.

The words that revealed the cruellest lie he'd fallen for. The words that had haunted him for so many years.

'You didn't really think it was your baby, did you, Daniel? You're not capable of fathering a child like a normal man. We both know that...'

But Jock looked...terrible, and Dan's first thought was that something had happened to Jenni. The sudden tightness in his chest came from nowhere and it was enough to make it impossible to pull his breath in any further. Slivers of potential grief were in there somewhere. And regret...?

'What's happened, mate?'

'It's Grace... She's had a fall. Fracture dislocation of her ankle. They're taking her up to Theatre any minute. Oh...' Jock rubbed his forehead with his fingers. 'That's why you're here? Are you going to be doing the anaesthetic?'

'Yes. I had no idea it was Grace.' There was something too close to relief to be felt now, which was disloyal of him, wasn't it? In the bigger picture, he knew Grace a lot better than Jenni. But his connection to Grace was through Jock. He might have met Jenni because of *her* connection to Jock but the pull that had been there between her and Dan was very different. And disturbingly powerful.

There was no outward hesitation to reveal that Dan was even aware of that flash of almost-relief. 'What happened?' he asked.

'She slipped getting off *Lassie*. Her foot got caught between the boat and the pier.' Jock gestured at the computer screen behind him. 'It's a Bosworth fracture. Wasn't apparent until the attempt at reduction failed and they took a new set of images.'

'That's where part of a fibular fracture is dislocated and trapped behind the tibia, yes?'

Jock nodded. 'At least the popliteal sciatic nerve block has given good pain relief.'

'How long ago was the accident?'

Jock checked his watch. 'Nearly three hours. Come on, I'll show you where she is. You'll be wanting to do a pre-anaesthetic check and get consent.'

'Yes…and Jock…?'

Jock looked back over his shoulder. 'What?'

'I'm sorry about yesterday.'

Jock dismissed the distraction with a single shake of his head. 'It's Jenni you should apologise to,' was all he said. He held Dan's gaze for a heartbeat. 'My sister doesn't lie. Ever.'

Dan could hear an echo of Jenni's voice now. *'I never lie,'* she'd said.

He'd believed it. It had only been a joke when he'd asked how he could know that *that* wasn't a lie.

Jenni was standing beside Grace's bed. She seemed to be avoiding making eye contact with Dan and he got that odd tight feeling in his chest again. Jock was right. He needed to apologise. She *had* to be mistaken. Maybe her periods were irregular anyway and if she'd had a dating scan, perhaps the technician who'd done it wasn't particularly proficient at their job and he was right in thinking that Jenni had already, unknowingly, been pregnant when she had arrived in New Zealand.

Whatever the reason for the error, Jenni clearly believed that he had fathered her baby, which meant she thought he had simply denied what was the truth as far as she was concerned. He had not only not offered her any kind of support, he'd all but called her an outright liar.

There was no getting away from it. Jock was right and he needed to apologise because he'd handled the situation very badly and he needed to fix it.

But not here. And not now.

'Hi, Grace...' He stepped closer to the head of the bed. Jenni stepped back from the other side and Jock took her place as he continued talking. 'You've done a bit of damage to yourself, haven't you? I'm sorry to hear that.'

Grace grimaced. 'It was such a stupid thing to do. I can't believe I've got to have surgery. I'm going to be off work for weeks...' Her eyes filled with tears. 'I've got so many women who need me.'

'They'll be taken care of.' Jock took hold of Grace's hand. 'You don't need to worry about that right now, sweetheart.'

'But there's nobody to take on the extra workload,' Grace said. A tear escaped and rolled down her cheek. 'That's why they were so keen to employ me. We're still short of midwives.' She turned her head to look directly at Jenni. 'You could stay, couldn't you?'

'No...' Jenni sounded as if the notion was ridiculous. 'I'm only here for a quick visit.'

'But your application for registration was accepted ages ago. You've got a work visa. You said that you might want to have a working holiday here one day...' Grace's voice cracked. 'Why not now? I *need* you, Jen. You *can't* leave.'

Dan picked up the chart on the end of the bed. He took in the latest observations of Grace's vital signs. Her blood pressure was up a little, but that wasn't surprising with the pain she'd been in initially and how stressed she was now. Had Jenni really jumped through the administrative hoops to get a visa that would allow her to work in New Zealand? Would she *want* to?

No... Of course she wouldn't.

Because she was pregnant.

And because *he* worked here...?

He expected to hear Jenni tell Grace that she

couldn't possibly stay. Part of him wanted to hear that she couldn't stay. He'd been alarmed at the idea that she might have been planning to emigrate even before he knew she was pregnant. Because he knew how hard it would be to stay away from her and he was so determined not to get emotionally involved with anyone again.

Ever…

But she didn't get a chance to say anything. They were interrupted by the return of the orthopaedic surgeon. 'We've got a theatre available. Ah, Dan…you're here. Are we good to go?'

'We will be in a minute or two. Grace, when did you last eat?'

'Lunchtime. Just a sandwich.'

'That was well over four hours ago now,' Jock added.

'Are you on any medications currently?'

'No.'

'Have you ever had a general anaesthetic before?'

'No…'

Grace had put her hand over her eyes but Jenni could see the tears leaking between her fingers. She'd never seen her friend this miserable.

Or her brother, for that matter. He was holding Grace's hand and being strong for her but Jenni could see past the outward appearance. He was worried sick. She could see the way he was gritting his teeth as he listened to Dan calmly asking questions about Grace's medical history, outlining the potential risks of anaesthesia and obtaining her consent for the procedure.

'Don't worry,' he finally told her. 'I'm going to look after you, Grace.'

Could Dan feel her staring at him? Was that what made him glance up and for their gazes to collide? Was he remembering that he'd said those same words the night they'd been left alone together, except that he had promised to look after *her*? What he had actually done was play a part in making sure her life was never going to be the same again, but now he wasn't prepared to even acknowledge that.

Except…

Was she imagining the impression, in that fleeting eye contact, that something might have changed since she'd dropped that bombshell on him yesterday? Had Grace been right in suggesting that it had been such a massive shock that Dan had simply needed time to absorb the news?

Not that it would change anything for her. The damage had been done.

It still stung that he hadn't given her a chance. That he'd decided she was lying to him and that was that. The connection she'd thought they had that night had been snapped and she'd prefer to have nothing more to do with Daniel Walker.

How could she possibly stay here, even if her

brother and her best friend might desperately need her to help them through this crisis?

But she couldn't leave either.

Not immediately, anyway.

She walked behind the bed as they took Grace up to Theatre and then waited with Jock in a staff area until the surgery was over. Jock was allowed to go and sit with Grace in Recovery.

'Stay here,' Jock told her. 'I'll come back and get you as soon as Grace is allowed to see you.'

But it was Dan who came into the lounge a short time later.

'Jock told me you were here,' he said. 'He asked me to tell you he might be a bit longer than he thought. He's going to stay with Grace until they take her up to the ward.'

Jenni nodded. Then she took a deep breath. This wasn't about her. This was about Grace. She could talk to Dan.

'How is she?'

'The surgery went well. They reduced the dislocation and the fracture and put in a plate and screws for the internal fixation. The surgeon was worried about damage to the ligaments but found they were intact when he was able to check them, so that's good.'

Jenni nodded again. She let out the breath she hadn't realised she was holding.

'She's been put in a tall immobilisation boot.

One of those fancy new ones made with a rigid plastic shell and heavy-duty Velcro straps.'

'A walking boot?'

'Yes, but she's not going to be able to weight-bear for at least four weeks. Could be three months until the fracture's completely healed.'

'Oh, *no*...' The realisation that there was no way she could walk away from this and head home any time soon was enough to make Jenni do what Grace had done earlier and put her hand over her eyes.

'What's wrong?'

Jenni shook her head. 'This is a bit of a disaster all round, isn't it?'

There was a long moment of silence and then she felt the cushions of the couch move as Dan sat down beside her.

'Will you stay?' he asked quietly. 'I heard Grace say that you've already sorted registration and a work visa.'

Jenni dropped her hand but didn't look up. 'Grace will be stressed enough that she's letting all the women on her list down and she'll hate not being able to help Jock with the house moving. She might try and do more than she should and end up getting complications with that fracture healing. And if *she's* stressed, Jock will be stressed.' She finally looked up to find Dan watching her. 'We're talking about my best friend. And my brother. I can't *not* stay, can I?'

'But…' Dan's hesitation pushed a button that Jenni didn't know she had.

Was he trying to find reasons why she shouldn't stay? Because he wasn't comfortable with the idea of having her around? Well…tough… This was *her* choice. Like the way she was going to raise *her* babies would also be her choice.

'It won't be a problem for me to get leave from work for a family emergency,' she said tightly. 'I've got friends who'll be happy to look after my house. And if filling in for Grace professionally works out and it's the best way I can help, I'll do that.'

Had Dan's gaze shifted to her belly?

'Being pregnant doesn't mean I'm incapable of working,' she snapped.

'I didn't say it did.'

'Some midwives I've known have worked until they were almost full term.' Jenni's tone was still cool. 'I'm sure Grace will be back on her feet well before I'm anywhere near that stage.'

Dan was looking down at his hands. He really was struggling with the idea of her being back in town, wasn't he?

But that hadn't been the impression she'd got when he'd first seen her, sitting on that step. He'd looked as happy as she'd felt to see him again. Almost as though seeing her had been the best surprise he could imagine…

She wanted to hang on to feeling angry with

him—maybe because she knew it might be harder to feel any other way—but it was proving difficult. She was starting to feel sympathy creeping in.

She could—and intended to—shut it out. She didn't want to start feeling sorry for Dan and make excuses for the way he'd reacted but she had pulled the plug on his life as he knew it, hadn't she? Not only that, she'd told him that something he believed was impossible was actually happening—that he was going to become a father.

Of course he needed time. She'd had the luxury of months to get used to all of this.

'It's okay, Dan,' she heard herself saying aloud. 'I might have come here to see you but that's not the reason I'm going to stay. I'm not going to make life difficult for you. Or ask you for anything. I'm quite prepared to be a single parent. To be honest, that's what I would prefer to be, anyway.'

Dan cleared his throat. 'I'm sorry,' he said quietly. 'About how I reacted yesterday. We should talk about that.'

Jenni could feel her lips curving into a smile, albeit a wry one. 'I suspect we'll have plenty of time,' she said.

Dan got to his feet. 'I'll go and see what's happening with Grace. I'm sure she'll be a lot happier when she knows that you'll be staying.'

Jenni watched him walk away. There was

something very different about his body language from when she'd seen him walking away from her yesterday evening. When he'd looked as if he couldn't get away fast or far enough. She was getting a sense that the shock was, indeed, wearing off. And that he was grateful for the room to breathe.

Perhaps they both needed that room to breathe. Was this yet another ace Fate had found to pull out of her sleeve? One that would force Jenni to think twice about shutting the father of her babies out of her life?

What if Dan got himself tested again and discovered that it wasn't as impossible as he believed?

That her children could end up having a father?

What if, when he knew he could believe her—and trust her—*everything* could change?

CHAPTER FOUR

'So you're Jenni...' Obstetrician Maria Gould was smiling broadly. 'I was delighted when Jock asked if I could keep an eye on you for the next few weeks. I didn't know he had a twin sister. And you're expecting twins yourself!'

'Thought I should keep up the family tradition,' Jenni joked. Maria was a senior colleague of Jock's, probably in her fifties, which gave her a rather welcome motherly vibe. 'Thank you so much for fitting me in.'

'No problem. Happy to help.' Maria opened the file of notes in front of her. 'Makes it a lot easier that you've printed off all your notes from your antenatal visits in Scotland. You've been in New Zealand for...nearly three weeks now?'

'Yes. I know I'm due for another scan and I should have come in earlier but Grace has been helping me keep an eye on my blood pressure and urine analysis and it's been crazy busy.'

'I'm sure it has. I knew Jock was due to move and then I heard about Grace's accident. I didn't realise you were visiting or that you'd come on board as a locum midwife.' Maria's eyebrows rose. 'How's that going?'

'My head's spinning,' Jenni confessed. 'The whole process was accelerated to give me a practising certificate so it felt like back-to-back interviews and assessments and orientation and…so much study. I spent several days in Wellington but I've still got online courses to finish in some areas. Midwives have more scope here than we do at home, with things like what medications can be prescribed, interpreting blood test results and making referrals and then there's all the cultural aspects that are important for Māori and Pasifika women that I need to get more familiar with. I'm loving the challenge, though.'

Because it had been demanding—and exhausting—enough to leave very little time to think about Daniel Walker. How lucky was it that she was in Wellington for her assessments at the time Dan had been helping with the house move? She'd only seen him in passing since she'd started working in the hospital, so it had been relatively easy to give him all the space and time he needed to come to terms with his impending fatherhood. To at least be prepared to find out the truth, at any rate.

What was taking him so long?

It was almost as if he still believed he couldn't

be the father of these babies, which meant that he still believed Jenni was lying to him.

'Jock sounds like he's thrilled with the new house,' Maria said. 'I hear he's got a private jetty for his boat.'

'It's gorgeous. Right on the shore, but still close enough to town to be an easy commute and it has road access.'

'So you're living there with them?'

'No. I decided to stay in the hospital accommodation. Grace is doing well on her crutches now and I wanted to give them time to settle into their first home together by themselves.'

That had kept her safe from being included in any time Dan and Jock were spending together out of work hours. As far as she knew, Jock hadn't tried broaching the subject because he'd agreed with Jenni that giving Dan some time to get to grips with the situation was the best way to handle this.

He's the kind of guy who'll shut down to protect himself. Disappear, even. I've seen him do it with women who want more from him than he's prepared to give... I suspect that getting away from something or someone was why he moved here in the first place.

'Fair enough...' It sounded like Maria was agreeing with the echo of Jock's voice but she was actually busy scanning her notes now. 'So they're definitely non-identical fraternal DCDA twins.'

'A boy and a girl.' Jenni nodded. 'Just like me and Jock.'

'The perfect instant family.'

'Mmm…' Jenni's smile felt tight. It was probably due to the way she and Jock had been raised. Or maybe she'd read too many stories about children finding their happy ever after endings. She'd certainly been left with the image that a *perfect* family would include a father…

'It makes your multiple pregnancy lower risk, as I'm sure you know. You'll be offered a planned birth at thirty-seven weeks but there's a sixty percent chance you'll deliver before then.'

'Grace will be back on her feet well before that so I'll be back in Scotland. Most airlines have a cut-off for international travel of thirty-two weeks for multiple pregnancies.'

Maria nodded. 'Remind me to give you a cover letter when you book your flights.' Her smile was sympathetic. 'It must be difficult being this far away from home…and your partner…?'

'I'm not in a relationship,' Jenni said.

Maria nodded but Jenni knew that saying she was single wouldn't prevent the assumption being made that the father of her children was someone who lived in Scotland. She knew about hospital grapevines and she was working in a new environment where she would be a subject of interest, especially as a noticeably pregnant midwife. She could imagine how Dan might react if any rumours got started. He'd run for the hills, wouldn't he.

That was a big part of why she wasn't about to push her way back into his space.

At some point, Dan was going to know the truth and they would have to interact in some way, even if they were living on opposite sides of the globe. How much better would it be for everyone involved if that interaction could be amicable, perhaps even friendly? However tempting it might be, burning bridges was only going to make it harder down the track.

Jenni still had what felt like plenty of time.

And she was more than busy enough during the day to make it easy to push any doubts aside and too tired at night to be kept awake.

'It's reassuring that your first trimester scan didn't show up any major anomalies. No growth discordance or markers for Down syndrome or spina bifida.' Maria's glance at the wall clock suggested she was aware of the time restraints of this appointment. 'I can't see any results for an amniocentesis or blood tests for other syndromes like Edwards' or Patau's.'

'No. I decided not to have an amniocentesis or chorionic villus sampling. Even such a small risk to the pregnancy wasn't one I was prepared to take.' She didn't need to confess how much she wanted to become a mother, did she? Or that she'd been planning to go to a sperm bank.

Maria just nodded. 'I'll schedule a second, anomaly scan for you, which should show us everything in much greater detail.' She reached for the cuff of the blood pressure monitor as she stood up. 'In the meantime, let's get on with the boxes we need to tick for today. You said you've got an outpatient antenatal clinic starting at nine o'clock and I'm due in Theatre, then for a hysterectomy.'

Dan got the call to the maternity department as he was starting to think about grabbing a quick late-morning coffee.

A woman who was thirty-seven weeks pregnant had been admitted for monitoring after having been found with markedly elevated blood pressure and higher than normal levels of protein in her urine at a routine antenatal clinic appointment. If the provisional diagnosis was confirmed to be pre-eclampsia, an early delivery was very likely to be recommended and part of the protocol was an anaesthetic consultation as soon as the patient was admitted.

Dan expected to find a registrar and/or the consultant for the obstetric team on call to be on the ward. He also expected at least one of the department's midwives to be looking after the patient.

What he didn't expect was to find Jenni McKay in the room.

Why not? He knew she'd started working as a locum to cover Grace being away with her badly broken ankle. He'd seen her more than once in the hospital over the last week or so, but he'd made no effort to have that talk he himself had said they needed to have.

Again…why not?

It wasn't as if he hadn't been thinking about how to approach what could be an awkward conversation. After Jenni had said she wasn't staying here because of him and that she wasn't going to ask him for anything, it seemed to confirm that there were options other than himself as the father of this child. If she was so sure it was him because she hadn't slept with anyone else around that time she would have had every right to ask him for financial support, at the very least. It would be stupid not to.

But did he really want to ask personal questions about Jenni's sex life in the period of time just before or after they'd had that ill-advised one-off passionate encounter themselves?

No…he really didn't. He also didn't want to analyse *why* he didn't want to talk about it, so he'd been doing what he was good at doing when it came to dealing with uncomfortable emotional issues in his personal life.

Backing off. Procrastinating. Waiting for the right moment.

Hoping that whatever the issue was, it might somehow magically disappear before it had to faced.

Not that this was the right moment, of course, but being this close to Jenni again was a wake-up call and it had made one thing suddenly very clear in no more than the space of a heartbeat.

He was being a bastard by giving the impression that he didn't give a damn.

Okay, he'd apologised for how he'd reacted when she'd told him she believed he was the father of her baby, but that wasn't enough, was it? He owed her more than that. And he owed it to his best friend to treat his sister better than this. They might have been able to put it aside during the hectic activity of shifting house, when Dan had hired a truck and helped Jock move all the second-hand furniture he and Grace had acquired, but, inevitably, it had to affect their friendship.

For just another heartbeat, Dan wondered what might be going through Jenni's head as she glanced up to see him come through the door of this patient's room, but there was no indication that she was taken aback. Quite the opposite.

She was smiling at him.

'Hi, Dan.' She turned back to the woman in the bed. 'Ashleigh? This is Dan Walker, the anaesthetist that Jock told you would be coming to see you.'

Jenni was looking completely at home in her new workplace, in her pale green scrubs, with a stethoscope dangling around her neck as well as an official lanyard. She reached up to hang the

cuff of the blood pressure monitor she was holding beneath the wall-mounted sphygmomanom-
eter and it stretched the front of her tunic against
her body. The bump of her belly was a lot more
noticeable than it had been a couple of weeks
ago and…yeah…she had that glow that pregnant
women often had in their second trimester.

Mind you, Jenni had had that kind of a glow the
first time he'd met her. It had been part of what
had made her so damned attractive…

'Dan? This is Ashleigh Perrin and her partner
Craig.'

'Hi.' Dan stepped closer to the CTG machine
beside the bed. Ashleigh had the discs strapped
onto her belly and he could hear the rapid beat
of an unborn baby's heart that was reassuringly
steady. He caught Jenni's gaze again briefly. 'Is
Jock still around?'

'He's gone to chase up the blood test results and
ultrasound report. He should be back any minute.'

Dan acknowledged the information with a
brief nod. He had already shifted his attention
to Ashleigh.

'How are you feeling at the moment, Ashleigh?'

'I feel fine,' she said. 'A bit of a headache,
maybe, but I never expected to end up in here.
I thought it was just going to be my last check-
up before I went home to wait to go into labour.'

'Blood pressure's come down with the first

dose of nifedipine,' Jenni said. 'Currently at one-sixty over ninety-eight.'

It was still high enough to be a concern. 'What was it initially?'

'It was one-ninety over one-oh-five when I took it in the clinic earlier.' Jenni's voice sounded commendably calm but Dan knew how alarming that reading would have been.

'Any visual disturbances?' Dan asked Ashleigh. 'Like blurred vision or bright flashes?'

'No.'

'Any abdominal or back pain?'

'No.'

'Any nausea or vomiting?'

'No…honestly, I feel fine, apart from this headache. I'm probably wasting your time. I'm not going to need an anaesthetic, am I, Jenni?'

'It's something to be prepared for,' Jenni said. 'As Jock said, we need to keep a close eye on your blood pressure, which is why I'm checking it every thirty minutes. We need to see what's happening with your blood tests and the ultrasound, but you're at a stage of your pregnancy where it's perfectly safe for you to deliver and, if that's going to be safer for you and baby, the best option will be to induce you. That's where Dan comes in. He'll be the one to give you an epidural anaesthetic.'

'But what if I don't want that kind of pain relief?' Ashleigh's expression was dismayed. 'We were planning to have a natural birth. In water. With the lights dimmed. We've got our playlist ready with all the music we've chosen and essential oils to burn.'

It was Jenni who caught Dan's gaze this time. She was wondering whether she should say any more or did he want to step in?

There was a lot he could say, but scaring someone when the objective was to try and lower their blood pressure was not going to be helpful. On the other hand, if this was severe pre-eclampsia, which could compromise the safety of both mother and baby, an urgent delivery would be the only option and that could end up being a Caesarean section.

Dan got the impression that Jenni was aware of the complications that could arise from the blood-clotting abnormalities caused by pre-eclampsia. A general anaesthetic was riskier because swelling of the airway could make intubation more difficult and the body's response to having a tube inserted could potentially be severe enough to cause a cerebral haemorrhage or pulmonary oedema. A neuraxial anaesthetic like an epidural was preferable but there might only be a limited window of time to place a catheter in the space around the spinal cord before platelet levels became too low and the risk of haemorrhage too great.

He held her gaze a heartbeat longer as he hesitated. Dan knew he was more than competent clinically at his job, but his now well-honed ability to keep a safe distance from other people—including his patients—meant that he was less capable of sensing emotional boundaries and danger zones. There was another level of discomfort trying to edge in here as well. An unprofessional one. He knew he could prevent himself from letting it affect him but the connection he had with Jenni McKay, along with all its emotional implications, was noticeably there.

Waiting in the wings...

To his relief, a split second later, he found he didn't have to say anything and that slightly disturbing eye contact was broken when Jock came into the room. He greeted Dan with a nod and then perched on the end of the bed, case notes open in his hands, to talk to Ashleigh and Craig.

Jock had a natural, almost cheeky charm that made him very easy to be around and Dan could understand why both Ashleigh and Craig had visibly relaxed in his presence. He also had no difficulty being empathetic but conveying all the information they needed to have. He was very good with people in both a professional and personal arena. He was, in fact, the best friend Dan had ever had and Jenni was so like her brother it was really no surprise that the connection he'd felt with her had been so instant. So powerful. He'd felt like he'd already known her for ever, hadn't he?

'So…' Jock was flicking through a swatch of test result papers. 'I'm not too concerned with the results of your blood tests although they need watching, especially your liver function and platelet levels. We'll repeat the tests later today. Your ultrasound examination shows that baby is fine at the moment but the rate of growth has slowed since your last scan and that could be due to the blood flow from the placenta to the uterus being a bit lower than we'd like.'

'What does that mean? Is it dangerous?'

'There's no danger at the moment but it could mean that it will be better for baby to be born sooner rather than later. That will certainly be the case if we can't get good control of your blood pressure. I'll be back to check on you a wee bit later, but Jenni's going to take good care of you till then.'

Ashleigh was smiling at Jock. 'It's really cute that you and Jenni are twins.'

Jock grinned. 'The red hair is a dead giveaway, isn't it? Or is it our accent?'

Craig laughed. 'Jenni told us.'

'We were talking babies…' Jenni patted her belly.

'And she told us she's expecting twins.' Ashleigh nodded. 'And how happy she is about that because she knows how great it is to *be* a twin.'

Dan had the odd sensation that he could feel

his blood draining out of his brain, making it difficult to join thoughts together.

Jenni was pregnant with *twins*? It shouldn't be that much of a surprise, given that fraternal twins ran in families, but it had just pulled the rug out from under some mental feet. That first impression that Jenni was far enough along in her pregnancy to make it obvious he couldn't be the father had just been blown out of the water.

It was instinctive to look at Jenni. To make eye contact to see if it was true. To try and make sense of the scramble of thoughts in his head.

Her gaze was so steady.

Calm.

Yes…her gaze told him. It's twins. And yes… she believed she had told him the truth when she'd told him he was going to be a father.

She'd just left out the bit about there being more than one baby.

That she was carrying what pretty much amounted to a small but perfectly formed family.

If only…

In that moment, before Dan took a deep breath and excused himself from the room for long enough to follow Jock and discuss this case in more detail, he was aware of how much he would have loved it to be true.

But it never could have been.

Because it might be an old-fashioned concept, but a *perfect* family had two parents. Two people who loved each other. And one of those people would never be Daniel Walker. He simply wasn't capable of loving someone like that again, so there was no point even thinking about it.

Oops...

It hadn't occurred to Jenni that a friendly chat with Ashleigh might lead to another bombshell revelation as far as Dan was concerned. Although, if he was so convinced she was lying and he wasn't the father, why would the fact that it was twins make so much of a difference?

But there'd been no mistaking the shock she'd seen in his eyes.

Distress even, and that had given her a strange squeeze in her chest that was definitely more than a stronger frisson of the sympathy she'd felt when she'd acknowledged her part in turning his world upside down.

Being angry with him and so disappointed in his reaction to her telling him she was pregnant had buried it, but it was peeping out again.

That extraordinary connection she'd felt with this man that had culminated in love-making that had felt like her soul was being touched as much as her body had been.

A fantasy of a relationship that could never be real because it was too intense…too *good*…to be true.

But Jenni could actually feel that distress she

could see in Dan's eyes right now, and that was making her chest feel tight enough to be painful.

Did he still believe that she wasn't being completely honest with him? That the truth was an impossibility? There had to be a reason why he couldn't or *wouldn't* let himself be persuaded that he could be wrong, and it was bigger than simply dismissing her as being a liar.

Much bigger?

And something he would prefer to keep private?

Thank goodness she had given him space since she'd announced she wasn't going home in a hurry. And that she hadn't tried pushing him when she clearly didn't know what else might be going on, because that might have guaranteed that she would never find out.

She wanted to find out.

Because that feeling of connection stayed with Jenni as the day wore on and there was only one reason why she was feeling so curious about what was going on in Dan's head.

Quite apart from him being the babies' father, she cared about him.

Ashleigh's blood pressure dropped a little further, stayed steady for a couple of hours but then, despite the medication, it began to rise again. Not only that, but Ashleigh began to experience more symptoms that were concerning enough for Jenni to call Jock.

'She's got epigastric pain that's new and she's feeling short of breath.'

'What's her blood pressure?'

'Rising. Five minutes ago it was one-sixty-five on a hundred.' Jenni could hear Jock whistle silently.

'Oxygen saturation?'

'Ninety-six on room air. Up to ninety-eight with some low-flow oxygen.'

'Are the latest blood results back?'

'I was just about to go and check.'

'I'll do that. I need to come and see her, anyway. We're going to need another IV line in and start some magnesium to prevent seizures.'

Things began to speed up after that and both Ashleigh and Craig quickly became alarmed enough at what was going on around them to discard their birthing plan in favour of getting their baby born as soon and as safely as possible. They agreed to induction and consented to a C-section if necessary. When the latest blood test results came back with elevated liver enzymes and a falling level of platelets the management of Ashleigh's labour stepped up another notch and Dan was called back.

'I know it's early in your labour and an epidural wasn't something you wanted but if we don't do it now, it may not be possible later on.'

'But what if I do need to have a Caesarean?'

'You'd have to have a general anaesthetic.'

'But then I wouldn't be awake for the birth...'

'No. And it's also safer for both you and the baby to have a spinal anaesthetic for a Caesarean.'

'Do it...' Craig sounded adamant. 'Whatever's the safest—that's what we want, isn't it, Ash?'

Ashleigh was crying. Her voice was muffled behind the oxygen mask that had replaced the nasal tubing. 'I'm scared...'

'We've got you.' Jenni moved in. 'We're all going to look after you, okay? Let's get you ready for the anaesthetic while Dan's getting scrubbed. We need you sitting sideways with your bottom right in the middle of the bed. I'm going to stand in front of you to help you stay in the right position.'

Seeing Dan gowned, masked and gloved for the sterile procedure made it easier to be this close to him as she stayed in front of Ashleigh with both hands on her shoulders to keep her still and hunched into a forward leaning position. It steered this further into professional rather than personal territory.

'This will be the worst bit, Ashleigh,' Dan warned. 'It's just the sting of the local going in. Count to ten and it will be fading.'

Ashleigh was hunched forward, her gown open to expose her spine, stained brown with the antiseptic it had been swabbed with. She had her head bowed so low her chin was touching her chest so it was easy for Jenni to watch Dan at work. He palpated the iliac crests on either side of Ashleigh's pelvis, with his hand outstretched so that his fingers were on the crests and his thumbs were feeling for the space between the lower lumbar vertebrae.

For just a nanosecond, things flicked for Jenni from being professional to being extremely personal.

Because she knew what it felt like to have Dan's fingers on her body and it was impossible to prevent the spear of sensation that seared her own nether regions. It didn't help that she had no part in this procedure other than to hold Ashleigh's shoulders and prevent any movement at critical moments.

'Stay still,' she reminded her. 'The sting should be starting to fade now.'

Jenni was hoping the sensation she was experiencing herself would also start to fade very soon but, if anything, as she watched Dan's deft movements as he discarded the syringe and needle he'd used for the local anaesthetic onto the sterile draped trolley and picked the specialised needle he needed to administer a combination spinal and epidural anaesthetic—the best option in case a Caesarean was needed—it seemed to be getting more intense.

Jenni knew what this was about. She'd talked to pregnant women for years now and she had listened to many confessions about the increased libido that could happen in the second trimester of pregnancy. She could explain why it happened, with the different levels of hormones circulating and the increased blood flow that was focused on supplying the uterus, that meant that the whole lower area of a woman's body could be more sensitive. Having your breasts get bigger, along with the rounded belly, could make you feel sexier too. It was one thing to share a conversation with other women, a giggle about an increased desire for sex and the shenanigans that were sometimes undertaken to satisfy it and even advice on the best positions to try when the bump was big enough to get in the way, but it was a very different matter to be experiencing it herself.

For someone with whom it had been a big mistake to have sex in the first place.

Even if it had been the best sex she'd ever had…

With an enormous effort, Jenni focused hard on the procedure and not the man doing it with such skill and efficiency.

She watched Dan insert the much larger hollow needle into the now anaesthetised gap between the vertebrae. She could feel his concentration as he carefully felt his way to the resistance that would let him know he'd reached the ligament just before the epidural space. He attached a syringe with saline in it, tapping it gently each time he advanced the needle a little further, until it emptied easily and let him know he was exactly where he needed to be. A long, thin spinal needle went in next, to administer drugs to a deeper level that would work fast and be effective for hours, and then it got swapped for a flexible catheter that would stay in the epidural space and could deliver medication via the port at the other end to keep the anaesthetic going as long as it was needed.

An adhesive sterile dressing went over the catheter on Ashleigh's back and the procedure was complete, fast enough to fit seamlessly between contractions. Not that Dan was going anywhere else in a hurry. He was drawing up more drugs as Jenni helped Ashleigh into a more comfortable position on the bed to breathe through her contraction and then took another set of vital signs.

It was much easier now to dismiss that unwelcome intrusion of something unacceptably personal that had happened only minutes ago. So recently that Jenni could still feel a twinge of it remaining.

That…*desire*…

For sex.

Not just sex.

Sex with Daniel Walker.

Something that should be the last thing she'd want to do with someone she had been so angry and disappointed with only a matter of days ago.

But there it was.

There was no way around the fact that she

wanted him. Just as much—no, probably *more*—than she had that first time.

Maybe it was just as well that it would be the last thing Dan would want to do with *her*.

Jenni had to reach past where Dan was beside his trolley with the syringes he was filling with medications and carefully labelling. He had taken off the gown over his scrubs so his arms were bare again and Jenni could actually feel the warmth of his skin as her own arm came too close to touching his.

Startled, she glanced sideways to find Dan had looked up from his task.

Just for a heartbeat.

But it was long enough for Jenni to feel a much sharper echo of that unacceptable sensation.

It was also long enough to see what looked disconcertingly like a reflection of what she was feeling in Dan's eyes.

Oh, dear Lord…

That connection was still there, wasn't it?

And, at a visceral level, it wasn't affected by anything else that was going on between them.

Because this was all about sex…

CHAPTER FIVE

THE PRIMAL GROAN was an indication of how much effort was being put into this push to help deliver a baby, but there was enough pain mixed in with the sound to be an indication that a top-up was required for Ashleigh's epidural anaesthetic.

It also felt weirdly like an echo of the way Daniel Walker was feeling at having to come back into this room. A few hours' respite hadn't really blunted the shock of the revelation that Jenni was pregnant with twins.

It wasn't so much the fact that she was carrying two babies that was messing with his head, though. It was that he'd been so prepared to use his observation that she had a bit more of a bump than he would have expected as confirmation that she was lying to him.

He felt ashamed of himself, to be honest. Part of that initial intense connection he'd felt with Jenni had been down to feeling safe with her. Knowing instinctively that she could be trusted as much as he trusted her brother.

But in the end he hadn't trusted her, had he?

So this felt awkward, especially when it was added to his avoidance of that conversation that was still hanging in the air as unfinished business between himself and Jenni. A perfect time to have that conversation was never going to turn up, so he was going to have to take advantage of the first private time that appeared.

Which wasn't going to be any time soon. They both had work to do.

Dan swiftly drew up and administered the drugs into the port on the end of the catheter and then found a spot where he could stay out of the way but keep an eye on his patient's vital signs every five minutes for the next half an hour or so.

Not that it was likely to take that long for the birth to occur as Ashleigh was well into the second stage of her labour. Dan would need to stay longer than that, however. Active management of the third stage in a woman with pre-eclampsia was important because there was an increased risk of a post-partum haemorrhage. Adjusting the anaesthetic for surgical intervention would be his responsibility if an urgent trip to Theatre became necessary.

In the meantime, he could see a monitor screen that gave him the figures for Ashleigh's heart rate and the automatic cuff was supplying a blood pressure recording every few minutes. He could count her respirations between contractions at least, and noting a sedation score was purely observation.

He could also watch Jenni McKay at work for the first time and she was so intensely involved with what she was doing she had no idea that she was also under observation.

'Breathe in deeply now, Ashleigh. Try and feel your tummy expanding. I'm just going to get another pillow between your legs, okay?'

Ashleigh made no response. She had dropped her head to lean into the crook of Craig's arm. She was lying on her side, her upper leg already supported by one pillow. Jock, gowned and gloved, was at the foot of the bed. Dan knew that the nearby covered trolley would have sterile kits available with equipment like forceps and vacuum cups for assisted delivery.

Jenni was rubbing Ashleigh's lower back after positioning the pillow and Dan saw her take a deep breath.

'Here we go…you've got another contraction starting. Keep your tummy out, breathe out really slowly through pursed lips and push down into your bottom. As hard as you can…that's great… you're doing *so* well… Keep it up, Ashleigh… Push and push and *push…*'

The broad Glaswegian accent was very familiar, thanks to having spent so much time with Jock since he'd arrived in Picton, and because of the friendship between the two men it also made him feel as if he was in good company.

Safe company…

There was more to listening to Jenni, however. The focus she had on Ashleigh—the encouragement and caring in her tone—was so compelling to listen to. Dan found himself unconsciously copying the breathing instructions. Watching the expressions on Jenni's face was just as compelling. She was demonstrating the breathing techniques, pursing her lips or taking a new breath, screwing up her face to mirror the strain of pushing and then her features would relax into a smile as she praised the efforts.

A look and then a swift nod passed between Jock and Jenni and Dan knew that the arrival of this baby was imminent.

'Don't push with this breath, Ashleigh. I want you to pant. Short breaths, like you're blowing out the candles on the biggest birthday cake in the world. Good girl…that's perfect…your baby's almost here…'

Dan couldn't look away. Everyone else in this room was watching this baby crowning and then sliding into the world but Dan hadn't shifted his gaze.

Jenni McKay was…

Stunning, that was what she was.

Not only physically beautiful, with that fiery red hair and pale, perfect skin and the brightest blue eyes he'd ever seen. She had this…glow… that came from within. Something fierce but gentle at the same time. Clever but still eager to learn.

Confident but vulnerable.

Things that should have been contradictions but seemed absolutely compatible.

She was intriguing.

So damned attractive it was dangerous.

The cry of the baby finally broke the moment, but not until he saw the huge smile that lit up Jenni's face even more and the sparkle in her eyes that could well have been caused by tears. She had a towel in her hands to take the slippery baby from Jock.

'He's gorgeous,' Jenni pronounced, smiling down at the baby as she held him for a moment to wipe his face with a corner of the towel. 'Such a bonny wee lad…'

She glanced up as she lifted the baby to put it on Ashleigh's chest, skin to skin, and caught Dan's gaze. She was still smiling. The kind of smile that went with the joy of witnessing the arrival of new life and the magic of a new family being created. Dan had seen it many times, of course, but he'd always managed to stay detached.

It had never felt like this.

He'd never thought he would feel this again, in fact. This…bone-deep yearning to have that family bond. To be a father.

He could imagine Jenni holding up one of her own babies like this. One of the babies that she said he was the father of.

He could imagine being that father. Feeling the relief of his son's safe arrival, the astonishment of this miracle of life happening before his eyes and…all the hope for a future that he'd only dreamed of having.

If only what Jenni believed to be the truth actually *was* the truth.

Dan had to stamp on that flash of a thought. It couldn't be allowed. He wasn't going to be sucked back into even hoping there was any possibility of it being true because that was the portal into a world that could feel so solid and secure and then simply disintegrate and mix your soul into the broken shards.

Jock was busy actively managing the third stage of labour. He had no idea he was handing Dan a lifeline when he handed him a labelled syringe to administer into the IV line he was about to flush to make sure it was still patent.

'This is some oxytocin we're giving you,' Jock told Ashleigh. 'It'll help with the delivery of the placenta and things should start to settle down for you after that.'

Dan let a long breath out as he slowly injected the medication. He could only hope that things might start to settle down for him as well.

* * *

Jenni was in no rush to go home, even though her shift had finished some time ago.

It had been a pleasure to be there to help Ashleigh and Craig with the first breastfeeding of their son and then catch up on what was some very detailed paperwork for a birth that needed careful medical management. Ashleigh was still receiving medication by IV infusion to control her blood pressure and prevent seizures so intensive observation was in place for the next twenty-four hours and a hospital stay of at least three days was recommended. It had taken some time for Jenni to provide a thorough handover for the nursing staff who would continue Ashleigh's care overnight and she finished up by calling Jock, who'd gone home over an hour ago. He was more than happy with the report on his most recent patient.

'You should go home and get some rest, Jen. It's been a long day.'

'I'm going now.'

'You're welcome to come here for dinner. Grace would love to see you. She's hanging out to hear how your appointment went with Maria this morning.'

'I've got a day off tomorrow. Tell her I'll bring some lunch and bore her with all the details. Right now, all I want to do is go home, have a long shower and blob out on the couch.'

Jock laughed. 'Fair play… See you later…'

Jenni left the birthing suite and maternity ward and headed for the corridor on the other side of the central space with the lifts and stairwell and a wall of windows that looked down on the gardens between the hospital buildings and the main road. Consultants' offices and on-call rooms were tucked into this space, along with the staff locker room, where Jenni had left her bag and clothes, including the comfortable trainers she needed to walk home in.

She was at the entrance to that corridor when she heard her name being called and she turned her head in surprise.

'*Dan...* You haven't been called to see Ashleigh, have you?' The beat of concern was for a complication from the epidural or spinal anaesthetic.

'No...'

'Have you got someone else in labour who needs an epidural?'

'No... I...was hoping to find you, actually.'

'Oh...' Jenni felt the thump of a missed heartbeat. Had Dan seen something in her expression earlier today? Had he felt the strength of those totally inappropriate thoughts about his body? She had to look away from him now, to make sure he didn't catch any lingering guilt about that. Or maybe to stop them coming back with renewed potency due to there not being any need to focus on professional responsibilities. There was no one else to hide any previous personal connection from either.

But Dan's expression was apologetic rather than accusatory. 'I keep waiting for the right time to talk to you,' he said. 'But I realised today that it's not going to magically happen unless I do something to *make* it happen.' His face softened into something close to a smile. 'So here I am, making it happen. Unless you need to be somewhere?'

Aye… Jenni needed to be standing in a long, hot shower, washing away the fatigue of a long day. Or lying on the couch with her feet up because she knew her ankles would be puffy by now after so much time on her feet with the extra weight she was now carrying. But this was important. And if she tried to walk away from Dan, Jenni suspected that her body would refuse the command.

The pull was astonishingly powerful. Magnetic…

'I'm done for the day,' she told Dan, letting her gaze flick back to catch his. 'I'm totally available.'

Oh, help…why on earth had she said something as ambiguous as that? She broke the eye contact and her line of vision shifted to the grouping of couches and chairs beside the windows. There was no one else taking advantage of the seating space or the view at the moment and Jenni would love to take the weight off her feet, but did she want to sit down next to Dan? What if her hor-

monally disrupted libido got even more out of
control and he could see a thought bubble over
her head that contained images rather than any
words?

The kind of images that Jenni had deliberately
kept fresh in her memory ever since that night…

She wasn't looking directly at Dan but she
could feel *his* gaze. She needed to escape, she
decided. But she'd just told him she was totally
available and with that instant of hesitation it became too late to change her mind.

'I wish you'd told me,' he said quietly. 'That
it's twins.'

One set of lift doors slid open behind Dan and a
kitchen staff member pushed one of the big stain-
less-steel trolleys that contained in-patient meals
into the foyer, coming closer to Jenni and Dan as
she turned it to head towards the maternity ward.

Jenni stepped further into the corridor to give
them the privacy that this conversation suddenly
needed and Dan followed her lead. The open door
beside her showed an on-call room that was unoc-
cupied. Perfect. She went inside and then turned
to face Dan, catching her bottom lip between her
teeth.

'I thought that you finding out that there's one
baby on the way would be enough of a shock to
start with.'

'I did think your bump might have been a bit
bigger than normal.' Dan cleared his throat. 'But

then I thought you might have put on a bit of weight so I couldn't say anything or that…or…'

'That I was further along in my pregnancy than I said I was?' Jenni lifted an eyebrow. 'Of course you did. You thought I was lying anyway, didn't you?'

Dan looked totally lost for words. Guilty. Confused, even?

'You still think I'm lying, don't you?'

'No.' Dan's head shake was sharp. 'I don't.'

He was saying something else, about Jock telling him that she never lied or that she'd said that herself, but the words were blurring for Jenni.

He believed that what she'd told him was true and that was all that mattered, wasn't it?

Except that she could hear the note of doubt in his tone. As if it was still too much of a stretch to really believe that he'd beaten the odds and been able to father a child. She could understand how difficult that would be to get his head around. Jenni was more than happy to do a non-invasive prenatal paternity test. It only needed a blood sample from her and a cheek swab from him and the comparison of DNA had an accuracy of nearly a hundred percent.

Or was that pushing Dan too fast and too far?

There was time to do this with more consideration, wasn't there? With some empathy for how huge this was for Dan.

'I know how unbelievable this must seem,' she

said. 'But…people do beat the odds. Some people even win the lottery. It might help if you got yourself tested again, Dan. Maybe the initial results weren't that accurate?'

He didn't believe any of that, she could see it in his eyes. But she could also see that doubt. The lack of comprehension and a good dollop of confusion. And…maybe even a little bit of hope?

It made him seem vulnerable.

It made her want to give him a hug.

To tell him that everything was going to be okay.

That she was happy to be having these babies and quite prepared to raise them herself. He wasn't going to have to do anything he really didn't want to do.

But then he surprised her. He was holding her gaze and his tone was as serious as his expression.

'A repeat test is worth considering,' he said. 'I'll make some enquiries about arranging one.'

It felt like a huge step had just been taken. Jenni found she couldn't look away from him. A wash of warmth that was a mix of relief and gratitude hit her like a small tsunami. She wanted to smile, but something was stopping her.

Another wave of sensation that had nothing to do with what they'd just been talking about.

It had nothing to do with anything that was going on with either of their lives outside of this room, in fact.

They'd both stepped back in time.

Oddly enough, it was back to that moment when Jenni had told him she never told lies. To that first moment when the connection between them had become something intimate and then overpowered everything else.

To that first kiss…

Maybe she did have a thought bubble that was visible and Dan could see the replay of that kiss that was filling her mind and fuelling the flames of desire flickering through her entire body.

Except he wasn't looking at the air over her head. His gaze hadn't shifted from hers and it felt as if Jenni was watching a replay of a whole lot more than that kiss in the depths of those sinfully dark eyes.

Not a word was spoken.

Dan used his foot to push the door of the room shut behind him and it closed with a definitive click that suggested the snib lock had fallen into place. And then he reached out with one hand as he stepped closer to Jenni, sliding his fingers around the back of her head to cradle it as he bent to cover her lips with his own.

Jenni heard herself make a sound like nothing she'd ever heard herself make before.

A sound of pure need.

She reached up with both arms to lock them around Dan's neck and stood up on tiptoes to press her body closer to his, not letting this kiss finish any time too soon.

She didn't want this to stop.

She wanted more. And she wanted it more than she'd ever wanted anything before in her entire life…

This really wasn't a good idea.

But Daniel Walker's body was having no trouble whatsoever in squashing that small voice in the back of his head that was issuing the warning.

He could even sidestep the pull into a part of his past he would never choose to revisit with the knowledge that he was making love to a woman who was carrying new life. It simply became part of a fantasy.

The perfect woman.

The perfect life.

The perfect sex…

Ultimately sensuous. Silent because there was nothing they needed to say aloud. They could communicate much more effectively with their bodies.

He hadn't forgotten the taste of Jenni's mouth, the heat of her tongue, the tendrils of fire her fingers created against his skin. What had dimmed, however, was just how explosive his reactions were and the difference in clarity was between memories and the real thing.

He had forgotten the tiny sounds she made as

he touched *her* that made him feel as if he was giving her the world. As if she wanted him more than she could ever want anything.

As much as he wanted her in this moment.

The single bed in this on-call room was far from ideal, but it didn't matter. The loose scrubs they were wearing were too easy to slip out of and…dear Lord, that roundness of Jenni's belly was the sexiest thing Dan had ever seen. Or felt… but it also generated a new kind of protectiveness that had never been a part of physical intimacy for him before.

Did Jenni sense that beat of pulling back as he tried to control the fall into the climax neither of them could resist? Maybe that was why she took the initiative and chose a position that would put no weight on her belly. On top of Dan, where he could hold her hips in both hands and watch her face as *she* fell…

And that was as perfect as everything else about this.

He had no idea how long it took to come back to earth. For his heart to stop pounding and his breathing to return to normal. About as long as it took for Jenni, it seemed, because he could feel her heartbeat as he lay behind her, spooning her with one arm over her body. It was only then that he realised he was holding her hand.

Or she was holding his?

It didn't matter who had initiated the hand holding. What did matter was that Dan had broken one of his golden rules that he could only indulge in sexual encounters when there was no risk of seeing each other again.

Living in the same place was enough of a red flag. Working in the same place was totally unacceptable.

Except…this still felt safe.

Was that because Jenni was still only here for a short time? That she was on holiday, albeit a working one?

Like the holiday she'd been on the first time they'd met?

She would be heading back to Scotland again soon.

So, yeah…this did still feel safe…

It was Jenni who broke the silence. With two simple words.

'Thank you,' she whispered.

Dan smiled. His fingers tightened around hers.

'You have no idea how good that was,' she added.

His smile widened. 'Oh, I think I do.'

Jenni broke their hand hold as she rolled to face him. She was shaking her head. 'No…you're not the one tormented by pregnancy hormones,' she said. 'It's astonishing what it can do to a woman's libido.'

Dan blinked. Was that what this had been

about? Just the sex, rather than anything to do with him?

Would it bother him if it was?

Yes…

No…

Who was he kidding? No man on earth would decline fantasy sex like that because someone was only interested in his body.

If anything, it only made it more perfect.

Even safer…

He cleared his throat. 'I hadn't realised that,' he said.

'It's not the same for everyone. I think I must have a bad dose.'

Dan could feel the breath of her sigh against his skin. 'Is it a problem?'

'It'll wear off. Give me another few weeks and it'll probably be the last thing I feel like.' Jenni's smile was pure mischief. 'Maybe I should make the most of it while it lasts.'

Dan was genuinely shocked, until he saw the gleam in her eyes that told him that this was an invitation.

A party that only he was going to be invited to.

They had been avoiding each other for weeks, thanks to the gulf of being blindsided and the swirling accusation and anger on both sides that made it impossible to find a way of closing that distance between them.

Well, they'd closed it now, hadn't they?

He'd only been planning to talk to Jenni. To try and suggest, politely, that a mistake had somehow been made.

What had made things change in such a dramatic fashion? Was it simply because they'd been alone and close enough for that overwhelming physical attraction to explode?

No. Of course it wasn't.

Dan knew perfectly well what had made that change. He could hear the echo of their earlier conversation.

'You still think I'm lying, don't you?'

'No... I don't.'

Should he have said more? That he believed *she* believed she wasn't lying?

Jenni had taken it to mean that he believed he was the father of her babies but he didn't believe that, did he? How could he?

She wouldn't either, if he went ahead and got that test and she could see the current results there in black and white.

In the meantime, was there any harm in being closer?

This close...?

Building a friendship, perhaps, that might mean they could part ways in the near future with no hard feelings on either side?

The internal discussion had happened in the space of no more than a heartbeat. Jenni was still giving him that look. Her naughty suggestion of making the most of her libido was still hanging in the air between them.

And Dan was smiling again.

'Let me know if I can help with that,' he murmured.

The soft gurgle of Jenni's laughter was as captivating as everything else about this woman.

'Mmm...' The sound suggested that the invitation might be rather tempting. 'I'll keep that in mind...'

CHAPTER SIX

'I'M PAST THE point of no return.'

'I suspect you were past that the moment you hooked up with Dan Walker.'

Jenni avoided meeting Grace's gaze. She hadn't guessed that something was going on again between herself and Dan, had she?

But Grace was smiling. 'You were definitely past it when you found out you were pregnant, weren't you?'

'That's true.' Jenni let out a relieved breath and opened the car's passenger door. 'I should have said I'm past the halfway point.'

'Well past, I would hope.' Grace laughed. 'You're nearly twenty-three weeks and twice that would be a ridiculous gestation even for a singleton.'

'I keep thinking of this as the twenty-week anomaly scan so it's usually halfway. I know I'm late but apparently it's helpful to leave the anomaly scan a bit longer for multiples. You can see more.' Jenni bit her lip. 'You don't mind coming with me, do you?'

'Are you kidding?' Grace handed her crutches to Jenni to stow in the back hatch. 'It's a treat to get out of the house and I can't wait to see the new members of the family.' But her smile was sympathetic. 'And I know it's a bit nerve-racking.'

'I just want them to be healthy. What if they've got congenital heart defects? That's the most common abnormality that gets picked up.' Jenni was watching Grace lift her injured foot into the car and got distracted as she saw her friend flinch. 'Your ankle's hurting, isn't it?'

'A bit. Maybe I was moving around too much yesterday. I got bored and sorted the kitchen boxes. And then I went down the steps to the jetty to have a look. Jock's been fixing it up ready to move *Lassie* from the marina to her new home.'

'Steps were not sensible.' Jenni shook her head as she peered at the parts of Grace's foot visible between the straps and casing of her walking boot. 'Aye…your toes look swollen. I think you need to get it checked out while we're at the hospital.'

'I'll see what Jock thinks. He's coming to the scan too, isn't he?'

'My instructions from the radiography department said I was allowed one relative or friend in the room.'

'You're a staff member. You can have anyone

you want in there.' Grace waited until Jenni had done up her seatbelt and started the car before she spoke again. 'Maybe it'll be Mandy doing it. You met her, remember? The night before you went back to Scotland.'

'How could I forget? Last time I saw her she was on the dance floor, joined at the hip and dancing with that Italian doctor who was supposed to be my date for the night.'

Aye…and Daniel Walker had been invited as a potential date for Grace. Talk about Fate having a bit of a laugh.

The beat of something awkward told her that Grace was remembering how that had worked out as well. She sounded slightly hesitant when she spoke again.

'Did you ask Dan if he wanted to come to the ultrasound?'

'No…' The suggestion was unexpected. 'I haven't even asked if he's booked another sperm test yet. I can't push him, Grace. He might believe I'm telling the truth but he obviously needs time to get used to the idea of being a father.'

'I reckon seeing his babies on the screen might be just the push he needs in the right direction. You're being too nice to him.' Grace's tone became puzzled. 'You've changed your mind about him completely, haven't you? You *like* him again…'

Jenni could feel the weight of the glance she

was getting. She kept her eyes firmly on the road as she started driving. She knew that 'like' wasn't the word Grace would have chosen if she'd known what had happened in the on-call room the other day but Jenni had only revealed that she'd talked to Dan—that he'd told her he now believed she hadn't been lying to him and that he had agreed to have another fertility test.

She'd told herself she was keeping the rest of that encounter a secret because things were complicated enough already, but maybe the truth was that she was being sucked into a fantasy world again.

A different one, this time. This wasn't about amazing sex with a gorgeous stranger she was never going to see again. This was about a fairy tale family, complete with a mother and a father and children who were the centre of their world, coming together and living happily ever after. She could almost imagine the tears of joy on Dan's face when they opened the envelope together that would give them the results of the DNA test with the truth there in black and white for the whole world to see.

It wasn't going to happen like that, of course. Jenni knew that. This was real life, with all the complications and emotional baggage that had the potential to cloud any major life event. Even if Dan did accept that he was the father of her children and decided that he wanted an active part in their lives, it wasn't going to lead to any kind of committed relationship.

Jenni might have changed her mind about becoming a mother but the aversion to getting married was still very much intact, thanks to the legacy her mother had left behind. She'd always found it so easy to fall head over heels in love and she'd always been so convinced that this man was 'the one'. That she was always going to be this happy and that life would finally be as perfect as she had dreamed it could be. Jenni and Jock had been only too happy to believe it too. Because life had been so much better when their mother was happy. Because what they'd wanted more than anything was a real family. To be loved and cared for. To be wanted.

It had always fallen apart, of course. And it had always been their fault. Jenni was never going to risk her babies believing they were responsible for their mother's bad choices and failed relationships.

Believing in the dreams of a 'real' family might be long gone, but indulging in them a little could be like a mood-enhancing drug and there could be a happier ending than she'd been beginning to expect. To have Dan acknowledge paternity and want to be part of his children's lives was worth being open to. Hoping for, even. To have him as part of her life, even if it was temporary, was…

Well…it was irresistible, to be honest.

That sex had been the best ever and, with the memory of the first time they'd made love, that was saying something…

It had been too long since he'd had an afternoon off.

So long, it seemed like the last time he and Jock had been out fishing together was only a distant memory. Dan glanced at the clock in the locker room as he finished changing into his civvies, wondering what time Jock might be finishing work today. Hadn't he said something, during the chaos of moving house and dealing with Grace's injury, about there being a few rotten boards on the jetty at his new place that needed fixing before he moved his boat? Dan could help with that. It might be a good way to check that their friendship wasn't being irreparably undermined by what was happening between himself and Jenni.

On the other hand, it might be better if Jock didn't know what had happened most recently between them.

Oh, man…

The *sex*…

Every man's dream. An unexpected sexual encounter that had been hot enough to smelt iron into steel. With a woman who was going to be out of the country in a matter of a few weeks, which made it almost possible to ignore the obvious strings attached.

For the moment, anyway.

Dan coiled his stethoscope, put it inside his battered leather satchel and hung the strap over his shoulder. He was ready to head home.

Except that he was still thinking about the sex and he certainly wasn't ignoring those strings. Because they'd added a whole new dimension to the experience. The physical things like the rounded belly and breasts that had such a delicious fullness to them were gorgeous but superficial. What was staying even longer in Dan's mind was the appreciation of something different about Jenni. A confidence, perhaps? Or a contentment? Whatever it was, she was in a space where she was in charge of her life and that was damned sexy all by itself.

She'd kind of been in charge of the sex too, choosing positions that were the most comfortable and some of those had been off-the-charts sexy.

Dan shut the door of his locker with a deliberate slam. Was he hoping the jarring sound would distract him before he needed to take a cold shower? It would definitely be a good idea to avoid Jock's company right now, he decided.

He should have known he was tempting fate.

He could almost hear a faint suggestion of cosmic laughter when he walked into the hospital's foyer to get to the main doors and found Jock, Jenni and Grace in front of the corridor that led to the radiology department. Dan wondered if it might be possible to pretend he hadn't seen them and keep heading outside, but Jenni's head was turning in that instant—as if she could feel his presence even though he was too far away to even call out a greeting.

And her face lit up as if she was delighted to see him.

Jock had seen that change in his sister's face as well and he turned his head to spot Dan, so there was no chance to sidestep this encounter. He needed to draw on his considerable ability to hide any inappropriate emotional reaction to anything around him. Like he did with every professional interaction he had. Yes…that was the way to go. Dan would act as if these people were a patient's family.

Or was one of them an actual patient?

Grace wasn't looking very happy at all She was pale and tired-looking and leaning heavily on her crutches. He could hear that she sounded upset as he got closer.

'I don't need a wheelchair, Jock.'

'You shouldn't be on your feet. Not until we know what's going on. You need an X-ray. Hi, Dan…' Jock was frowning. 'What do *you* think?'

'About…?'

'Grace's toes.'

Dan dropped his gaze but it was an effort when what he really wanted to do was make eye contact with Jenni. He wanted to know if it had been his imagination that made it look as though she was so pleased to see him. If it wasn't, he wanted to know if there was any chance she would like to see him alone.

And *when*…

It was a good thing that he needed to look at Grace's toes.

'They look like sausages,' he said.

Jock huffed with laughter. 'That's your professional opinion, is it, mate?'

'What are the limb baselines like?'

'Haven't had a chance to find out.' Jock glared at Grace. 'I was about to take Grace into Emergency and get someone to page whoever's on call for Orthopaedics.'

'I'll do it later,' Grace said. 'I'm not going to miss going to Jenni's scan with her. She's nervous enough as it is.'

Something dropped in the pit of Dan's stomach. He caught Jenni's gaze but any questions he might have wanted answers to had evaporated completely.

'Is something wrong?'

She shook her head. 'Not at all. I'm just here for the twenty-week anomaly scan. A belated one,' she added hurriedly, as if she knew Dan was trying to make sense of conflicting information on the stage of her pregnancy.

'But you're nervous?'

She shrugged, her smile a little embarrassed. 'There are times when ignorance is definitely bliss. I seem to have a long list of birth defects and genetic abnormalities that are chasing each other around in my brain.' She turned back to Grace. 'You should absolutely go and get your ankle checked.'

'I can do it later, after your appointment.'

'What if it's a blood clot? You're not going to collapse with a pulmonary embolism in the middle of my scan, thanks very much.'

Grace looked torn. 'Jock can go with you, then. I don't want you doing this alone.'

But Jock was also looking torn. And slightly paler at Jenni's suggestion of a serious complication with Grace's ankle fracture.

'*I* could go with you.'

The words were out of Dan's mouth before he could stop them and they fell into a silence that was sudden enough to make it very clear that they were all aware of the significant undercurrents here.

What had he done?

Wow…

For a heartbeat, Jenni was completely shocked. Was this it? Dan stepping up to acknowledge that he was the father of these babies? That he was invested in their wellbeing and he wanted to be a part of their lives?

Why else would he want to see them before they were born?

Jock and Grace were looking a wee bit stunned as well.

Even Dan looked as if he couldn't quite believe what he'd just said.

But the moment passed almost as instantly as it had arrived as Jock's lips curved into a smile that suggested the perfect solution had been found.

'Good on you, mate,' he said quietly. Then he turned back to Grace. 'Don't move,' he ordered. 'I'm going to get a wheelchair from Reception.'

Movement helped dilute the undercurrents. Jenni helped get Grace settled into the wheelchair and then the small group broke up. Jock wheeled Grace towards the emergency department and Jenni and Dan walked into Radiology.

'I'm Jenni McKay,' Jenni told the receptionist. 'I've got an appointment for an ultrasound.'

'Ah…yes. You're with Mandy. She told us you were coming. You're Jock McKay's sister, aren't you?'

'I am.'

The receptionist shifted her gaze to Dan. Jenni's heart sank as the young woman's eyebrows rose. Dan must have known he would be recognised in his workplace. He'd also know how fast a rumour would get around a hospital. Jenni felt suddenly protective. Dan was taking a huge step here. He didn't deserve to be the subject of generalised gossip at the same time.

'Jock was going to come with me,' she told the

receptionist. 'But he's caught up. Dan offered to come instead—as a friend. My instructions did say I could bring a family member *or* a friend.'

'Okay…yes, that's fine…' The slightly disappointed tone told Jenni that she'd been successful in diverting attention from Dan. 'Take a seat and you'll be called soon.'

The receptionist might be disappointed but the glance from Dan told Jenni that he appreciated his privacy being respected.

As much as Jenni appreciated that he was here with her?

Two parents, about to get a peek at their unborn children?

She didn't mind keeping it a secret at all. They both knew the truth and that was what really mattered.

The ultrasound technician, Mandy, accepted the same story that Dan was just filling in for Jenni's friend and brother to keep her company.

'I get it.' She nodded. 'Everybody's nervous of this scan so it's good to have someone with you.' She smiled at Jenni. 'Must be hard doing this bit alone—so far from home. I'll get lots of pictures for you so you can share them with everyone.'

'Thanks so much…that will be great.'

Jenni was settling back on the pillows. The big screen on top of the ultrasound machine was tilted in her direction. Mandy sat in front of it with another screen amongst all the controls, squeezed some gel onto Jenni's abdomen and then picked up the transducer. She grinned at Dan.

'You don't have to stand in the corner,' she said. 'Come and sit down. It's not that scary. You might be doing this for real one day, you know.'

Dan said nothing, but sat down on the chair on the other side of the bed, which put him right beside Jenni's head. It was a position that made it easy for the extra person to see the screen clearly. It was close enough for it to be easy for the father of the baby to hold the hand of the mother-to-be.

This was as close as he was ever going to get to doing this 'for real'. If he let himself, just for a few minutes, he could pretend it *was* real, but he wasn't about to do that.

No way...

For a while, it was easy. Fascinating, in fact, as Mandy expertly manoeuvred the transducer until she got the view she wanted and then froze images on her screen for a few seconds, swiftly shifting cursors to mark points and measure parameters. She was good at her job and gave them as much information as she could—probably a lot more than she would have with patients who weren't medical colleagues.

'They probably used the crown to rump length of the smaller twin to establish gestational age in your first trimester scan, but it's less accurate in the second trimester. The measurements are still within an acceptable range for variation, though. You don't have an accurate date of your last menstrual period, do you?'

'No. I've never been that regular and I think that international travel and jetlag might have disrupted things even further.'

'Jetlag is horrible,' Mandy said. 'Must have been worth it for such an amazing trip, though, right?'

'It was a memorable trip,' Jenni agreed.

'And you're back again already. Can't keep away from us, huh?'

'Something like that, aye…'

Jenni had her lips pressed together as she let her gaze slide sideways to Dan in a brief flicker of eye contact. It looked as though she was trying not to smile—with that hint of a suggestion that making love with him again might be too tempting to resist. The same kind of smile she'd given him in the on-call room when he'd offered to help her with her out-of-control libido.

Dan felt one of his eyebrows flicker as he tried to send back a silent message.

Just say the word, babe… I won't say no…

Why would he? In the big picture of his life, this was just a few pixels. A few weeks and then it would be nothing more than a very pleasant memory.

The perfect kind of relationship as far as Daniel Walker was concerned.

The only kind, in fact.

And he'd regained his normal level of emotional control. Look at him now—keeping a safe, clinical kind of distance even while negotiating an emotional minefield of disturbing memories, broken dreams, accusations and mistakes.

Mandy was back in clinical mode too.

'Okay…look…this is a four-chamber view of Twin A's heart. We can see normal anatomical structure and ventricular function. Heart rate's also normal at one forty beats per minute. Looking good…'

No abnormalities were seen with either twin's heart. Or their brains. They both had two kidneys and no hint of malalignment or other issues with their spines. Minutes ticked past to become an hour and kept going. The position of the placentas had been confirmed, and the gender of the babies.

'One of each.' Mandy nodded. 'Perfect.'

Twin B made it difficult for Mandy to locate a view to measure the length of both a femur and a humerus. She focused on the screen as she repeatedly shifted the transducer and the silence grew until it was uncomfortable.

Dan was starting to wonder if he could slip away at some point soon. Maybe Jock, with or without Grace, would turn up and be able to take over keeping Jenni company? He wasn't really paying attention to the blobs on the screen when they shifted and morphed into something new so he certainly wasn't expecting to have one of those emotional mines detonate right in front of him but…there it was…

A tiny hand that was moving as though it was waving at him. He could see the miniature fingers clearly enough to count them. He could almost feel what it would be like to have them closing around his own finger and the curl of sensation that speared his chest took his breath away.

This was the tiny hand of a real person and suddenly this became a fantasy moment—a glimpse into what his life could have been like if it hadn't fallen apart in such a spectacular fashion.

He must have made a sound. Or perhaps Jenni had the ability to sense his emotions even when she wasn't looking at him, because she turned her head in that split second and caught his gaze. Just for a heartbeat before she was drawn back to that screen, but it was long enough for it to become part of the fantasy—as if they were both looking at the hand of one of their own babies.

Except that this crossed the boundary between fantasy and reality, didn't it? Because Jenni actually believed this *was* his baby's hand that he was seeing for the first time. If Dan wanted to, he could step into that space and be the father he'd always dreamed of being. He could decide not to get himself tested and, as infinitesimal as the possibility was, he could let himself believe that a miracle *had* happened. He could suggest to Jenni that no DNA tests really needed to be done. He could become a part of her life and help her raise the twins—as their father. Perhaps they could even get married and live happily ever after?

Except they would all be living a lie, and that would be unacceptable for everybody involved.

But…and the thought came so unexpectedly it stole Dan's breath.

What if they didn't have to lie?

What if it was all out in the open right from the start?

If it didn't actually matter that he wasn't the father?

People had found ways around their inability to have their own children for ever. Babies were adopted. Surrogates could be used. Assisted fertility with sperm or egg donations if necessary were commonplace these days. If his marriage hadn't imploded perhaps that was how Dan would have achieved his own family in the end. But he'd felt betrayed enough to never let anyone close enough again to form the kind of relationship that would be a strong foundation to share parenthood.

Did he feel safe enough to let Jenni that close? *Maybe…*

Could he be a father to children that weren't biologically related to himself? Love them as if they *were* his own? Judging by the way he'd felt when he'd seen that tiny hand on the ultrasound screen, the answer to that question was a resounding 'yes'.

The prospect of his life changing to that degree was everything he could have dreamed of.

But the prospect of it all going horribly wrong was scary enough that it would make it easy to back away.

The scales were tipping. One way and then the other. With fear on one side and a bone-deep yearning on the other.

Dan pulled in a deep breath that felt shaky.

Jenni must have heard—or felt—that wobble. When she glanced up at Dan, this time, she had tears in her eyes. That she was as overcome with emotion as he was created an astonishingly powerful connection.

He hadn't realised that he had his hand resting on the side of the bed until Jenni's fingers touched his. She had already turned back to the screen but she didn't take her hand away. Her fingers curled around his to cup them gently and Dan didn't take his hand away as he also shifted his gaze back to the screen. He could see the rest of the arm now and the image stilled as Mandy clicked to measure the bone length between the elbow and shoulder. He could see the baby's head in profile, with a tiny button of a nose and a mouth that he could imagine was smiling.

Dan could feel his own lips curving and he had to swallow a lump in his throat. He closed his fingers around Jenni's so that he was holding her hand properly.

Those scales had stopped rocking.

Yearning had won, at least for now. Maybe that was because there was nothing permanent about this. The clock was ticking and it was only a matter of time before everything changed again. This window was the only time that Dan would ever have to be this close to the dream.

And that was huge.

The fear had simply been outweighed.

CHAPTER SEVEN

'YOU'RE GETTING STARED AT. *We're* getting stared at.'

'People find obvious pregnancy fascinating for some reason. Maybe they think there's a chance I could go into labour or even give birth in a public playground.' Jenni offered Dan a slightly apologetic smile. 'And I guess they assume we're a couple so we're walking around advertising the fact that we have sex occasionally.'

Dan laughed. 'Want to sit down for a minute?' He gestured towards a park bench that was currently empty. 'We're going to be too early for dinner even if we take a detour to the beach on the way.'

Jenni was quite happy to sit and rest. She loved this area of Picton with its majestic palm trees on the edge of an area that was a community magnet on a sunny late Sunday afternoon. People walked dogs or pushed prams on the pathways, sat on the grass in the sun to read a book or have a picnic and, most popular—there was a children's playground that even included a huge pirates' ship to climb on and play inside.

'Playgrounds have changed since I was a kid,' Dan said. 'We were lucky to have a row of swings, a slide and a seesaw.'

'Did you have those witch's hat things in New Zealand? Where you sat or stood on a narrow wooden edge and hung onto the spokes and it whirled around and went up and down at the same time.' Jenni blew out a breath. 'I was terrified of them.'

'I remember an iron horse,' Dan told her. 'With bars to hang onto in front of all the metal saddles in a row. It was on springs and you could make it rock hard enough for someone to lose their grip and go flying. All good fun—unless you were the one who got bucked off.'

'Did you have brothers and sisters to go on the horse with you?'

Jenni felt almost shy asking the question. There was too much she didn't know about the father of her children so it was lovely to be getting into the habit of spending more time with just the two of them. Getting to know each other better as Dan began to let his guard down and talk more. Right now, they were on their way to the Brazilian barbecue restaurant that had been where they'd met for the very first time. Just them. They hadn't invited Jock or Grace.

Dan didn't seem to mind the personal question. 'No,' he said. 'But I had lots of cousins. I got brought up by an aunt on my mother's side of the family, after my parents died in a car crash. Big Pasifika families always seem to have room for one more...' He hesitated for a moment. 'But I was just one in a crowd. It wasn't quite *mine*, you know...?'

'I do know,' Jenni said quietly. 'It must be a bit like being in a foster home. Even if the families we went to seemed like they genuinely wanted me and Jock to be there, we never felt like we really belonged.'

Dan nodded. 'That's why I wanted to get married and have a bunch of kids. A big family that was all mine.'

'And I went in the opposite direction and decided to never even try to have a family.' Jenni laughed. 'Look at us now.' She put her hands on the mound of her belly. 'They're having a bit of a party in here.' She reached out and caught Dan's hand and put it where her hand had just been. 'Can you feel that?'

Dan's face went very still and then his lips curved in a gentle smile as he spread his fingers to feel the ripples of the baby moving beneath them. The first time he'd done this had been when they were in bed together, just after Dan had come to that ultrasound scan with her. When things had changed between them.

This wasn't simply about the sex any longer. Maybe it was because her pregnancy hormones were changing and that flush of libido was fading. Or—and Jenni suspected this was the real reason—it was the feeling that they were becoming a real couple. That the relationship they were forming between each other was just as important as the bond Jenni was hoping would form between her babies and their father.

Not a real couple in the sense of it being a permanent relationship, of course—like a marriage—but still a couple.

Two people who had created children together.

Parents that would have a bond that would last for a lifetime.

Friends…?

A woman walked past the bench and noticed Dan's hand on her belly. Her smile suggested that she knew they were a lot more than friends and Jenni felt herself catch her breath. They weren't a *real* couple. She knew what happened when you believed that a perfect future depended on being a real couple.

Dan's hand slipped off her belly as she got to her feet.

'I'm starving,' she announced. 'If we turn up, I'm sure they'll let us have our table a bit early. I don't want to be out late, anyway. Early start tomorrow. Grace is coming in to do her first antenatal clinic since the accident.'

* * *

'Grace…you're back! I'm so happy to see you.'

'My first day. And I'm just very part-time for a while. I'm testing my ankle by helping Jenni with the clinic this morning. How are you, Lynn?'

Lynn handed her urine sample to Jenni. 'Counting the days. I told Chris this morning that he gets to have the next kid in this family.'

'He's not with you today? It's been too long since I last saw you both.'

'I know. We were so disappointed when we heard about your accident and that you might not be with us for the birth. No offence, Jenni.'

'None taken.' Jenni was unscrewing a jar to get a dipstick.

'He couldn't make it today—urgent appointment with one of his clients. I told him he didn't need to come. This is the perfect pregnancy and nothing is going to go wrong.' Lynn beamed at Grace. 'Do you think you'll be properly back on deck for our big day? Will four weeks or so be enough time?'

Jenni gave Grace a stern look. 'Only if she follows the rules. She overdid it a while back and ended up in Emergency with a foot that looked more like a foot*ball*.'

'Oh, *no*… Ankles can be tricky, can't they?'

'It's fine,' Grace said. 'They had to check that the alignment of the fracture repair was still okay, but it came right after I kept my weight off it for a few days. I'm walking well now, but I can only increase the time on my feet gradually. With a bit of luck, I'll be able to be with you and Chris when your baby arrives.'

'And if you're not? Will you still be here, Jenni?'

'I'll keep my fingers crossed, but it might be cutting it a bit fine. I haven't booked my tickets yet, but I'm almost twenty-eight weeks now and the cut-off for flying when you're carrying multiples is thirty-two weeks.'

'You're nearly as big as me.'

'I'm starting to feel it,' Jenni said. 'Not that I'm ready to slow down yet, but my ankles can be very puffy by the end of the day. It's probably a good thing I'll be job sharing with Grace from now on. Now…let's get you up on the bed and Grace can do your tummy check.'

Jenni took the opportunity to sit down for a moment then, noting the normal result of the urine analysis in Lynn's notes. Unconsciously, she found herself feeling for the upper border of her own uterus when Grace was doing the same on Lynn's exposed belly as she began the abdominal examination.

The strong kick and then another from the small feet beneath Jenni's hand made her smile.

It had made Dan smile yesterday too, hadn't it? And not just at the playground.

Jenni closed her eyes as she let out a slow breath,

letting herself sink back into the pleasure of their time together after they'd been out to dinner.

The sex had been very gentle.

Very slow.

Unbelievably delicious…

He had spooned her for a while afterwards, with his arms around her, both hands cradling her bump in the hope of feeling the babies moving again, but he hadn't stayed the night.

He never did.

Because they weren't a real couple. Neither of them wanted to be.

And Jenni would be going home to Scotland very soon.

She still felt safe.

When she opened her eyes again, pulling herself back into the present, Grace was lifting the tape measure she had stretched across Lynn's belly and swapping it for the foetal Doppler to check the heart rate.

'Fundal height thirty-seven centimetres and heart rate is one-seventy,' she told Jenni, who noted it. 'Your baby's following every rule in the book,' she told Lynn.

The rest of the antenatal visit went just as smoothly and then Grace took a seat at the desk and put her foot up on another chair.

'You should have your feet up too,' she told Jenni.

Jenni laughed. 'We'd look a right pair if someone came into the room, wouldn't we?' She picked up her pen. 'Let's get these notes sorted. I think you've been here long enough for your first day back.'

'Ooh... I like having a secretary.' Grace leaned back in her chair. 'Lynn Grimshaw, primigravida, thirty-seven weeks. On examination, abdomen gravid, appropriate for dates, linea nigra present. On palpation—a singleton foetus, longitudinal lie and cephalic presentation.' She was smiling. 'I've missed this.'

'What—all the paperwork? Or being at work?'

'Being at work with *you*.' Grace held Jenni's gaze. 'I don't want you to go back to Glasgow, Jen.'

'But I have to.'

'Why?'

Jenni blinked. Surely the answer was obvious? 'Because it's home.'

'But isn't home where the heart is?'

'And my heart's in Scotland,' Jenni said. 'Where I grew up. Where Jock and I both grew up knowing what it was like to never feel like we had a real home. I'm not going to let my kids feel like that. Ever. And I don't have to. I've got a house there. I've got a job to go back to.'

'But you've got family here. Your brother. And *me*...'

'You guys might decide to come back to the UK one day.'

Grace shook her head. 'We love it here. We're actually going to go and talk to someone about applying for permanent residency and, hopefully, citizenship down the track.'

Jenni's heart sank. She'd be living on the other side of the world from the only real family that her children had, apart from their mother. If she added their father into the lineup, it was starting to feel...wrong...?

'You're going to need all the help you can get when these babies turn up.' Grace's tone held a plea. 'Who better to do that than their uncle and auntie?'

'I can't stay here to give *birth*...' Jenni shook her head to underline how unacceptable the suggestion was. 'I've got to get home well before they're due. I've got a lot of organising to do. Bassinets and nappies and clothes and goodness only knows how many other things.' She blew out a breath. 'I'd better start making some proper lists. And book my tickets home. How did I think that I had plenty of time and I could just ignore it all?'

Because she'd been floating along in the very unexpected new relationship kind of bubble she'd found herself in with Dan?

Aye...doing something as practical as booking her flights home would have burst that bubble in a hurry.

They'd both known that it was temporary, of course—that was part of the reason they had allowed themselves to indulge in the pleasure of their attraction to each other, wasn't it? But the reminder of the cut-off point for international travel for pregnant women this morning had been a wake-up call that the end was rapidly approaching.

The clock was ticking quite loudly, in fact.

And that was a bit of a shock, to be honest.

Grace must have seen how disconcerted Jenni suddenly was.

'Sorry, I didn't mean to stress you out.' Grace made a face. 'Hey… I've got lists that we give to first time mums on their initial antenatal visit. I'll print you a copy.'

'Thanks. Are you coming in tomorrow?'

'Yes. I'd like to come with you for the home visits you've got scheduled and see how well I do with different houses and steps and so on.'

'Good plan. But you need to be honest if it gets too much for your ankle and I'll drop you home. Overdoing it at this stage would be silly.'

Grace made a face but nodded her agreement and then smiled. 'And you're coming to dinner, remember? Jock and Dan have a day off and they're fixing the last bit of the jetty and then they're going to go and get *Lassie* and bring her home. If the weather stays this nice, we might have a picnic on the beach.' She was watching Jenni carefully. 'That's not a problem, is it? Having an evening with Dan?'

'Um…no…' Jenni cleared her throat. 'We've actually been getting on quite well recently…'

Perhaps it was the tone of her voice. Or the certain type of smile she couldn't suppress. Or maybe her friend just knew her too well, because Grace's eyebrows rose sharply.

'*How* well?' She was still staring at Jenni. 'Oh, my God…are you *blushing*, Jenni McKay?'

'I never blush.'

'You blush all the time. You're a redhead.'

'So's Jock. I've never seen *him* blush.'

'He's a boy.' Grace was still smiling. 'I wonder if Dan's going to tell him what's been going on?'

'I doubt it. It's not as though it's anything significant. We're just…friends, I guess.'

Grace's smile faded. 'You're a bit more than friends.'

Jenni broke the eye contact. 'Aye, well…we've got a bond that's going to be there for the rest of our lives. It will be better if our relationship is amicable.'

Amicable…? That was a bit of a joke, given how close they'd been—again—only last night.

But Grace didn't pick her up on her word choice. Her brow was furrowed now, as though she was worried about something.

'Maybe that's the best reason of all to have your babies here,' she said quietly. 'To let their father bond with them.'

Oh, *help*…

Jenni could feel a prickle of sensation on her skin right now—as if Dan's hands were on her belly again, the way they had been last night. She could feel his pleasure in feeling the ripples and bulges of the movement of the tiny bodies beneath her skin. How much more intense would it be for him to be actually touching—and holding—his babies in their first moments of life?

She would be denying him that experience.

And that was definitely something she could start feeling guilty about.

This was like old times.

Before life had been tipped upside down.

To one side, Daniel Walker could see the white-tipped ripples of the wake Jock's boat was making as they left the marina behind and gained some speed. If he turned his head, he could see Jock at *Lassie*'s wheel, focused on the route he was taking to get his boat home to tie up at his own jetty.

They'd spent all day working on the jetty. They'd removed some decking boards to replace the last rotten beam and rafters beneath, replaced the decking boards and then finished with a coat of timber stain. They'd carried the portable barbecue and a chilly bin full of beers down the steps to the small private beach and then set off to collect *Lassie*. The jetty would be dry and the beers still cold by the time they got back to enjoy the picnic dinner planned for later.

'Have we got time to stop and catch a snapper to go on that barbecue?'

Jock threw a look over his shoulder. 'Sadly, no. But Grace has got some fancy sausages from that gourmet butcher in town for us tonight.' Jock grinned. 'It's one of our favourite dinners. I reckon she started falling in love with me when I fed her their traditional British bangers.' He was looking straight ahead of the boat again now but Dan could still hear him clearly. 'Jenni's coming over. She'll be there by now...'

Something tightened in Dan's gut with an extremely pleasurably twinge. Okay, maybe this wasn't really like old times, when he and Jock would spend a day out fishing and then share a dinner at the old villa that was the hospital accommodation for temporary or new staff members. Jock was engaged to the love of his life and Dan was helping him sail his beloved boat to the property of his dreams, where he was going to live happily ever after.

And Dan was having a fling with Jock's sister, for heaven's sake. Getting steadily closer to a woman who was pregnant with twins that she believed were his own children.

He was being offered the opportunity of getting as close as he'd ever dreamed of getting to living happily ever after himself. And the time together last night, when he'd felt the movement of the babies as clearly as if the barrier of Jenni's skin had evaporated, had stayed with him today. He could still feel the tingle of it in his hands.

So life couldn't be any more different really, could it?

Not that he was committing to anything yet. He was taking one day at a time. One magic night with Jenni at a time, because that was all that he could allow himself to do. What would make it perfect, of course, would be if they fell in love with each other, but how likely was that to happen? Jenni had told him she was quite prepared to be a single parent—that she would, in fact, prefer it. And for himself, well…the kind of trust you needed to fall in love had been so broken for him, it could never be the same. It might not even be a possibility.

But that didn't necessarily mean it was impossible to find something you could trust enough to rest a future on, though.

Did it?

It felt like that question was being answered only a short time later, when Jock slowed *Lassie*'s engine and Dan got ready with the ropes to tie the boat up as they came into the jetty and he could see Jenni and Grace waiting for them.

When the smile on Jenni's face gave him that spear of sensation in his gut again, and this time it spread its warmth right through his body.

Yeah…it felt like he could trust someone who smiled at him like that.

Life was different all right.

Better...

So much better...

The small beach was framed by Pohutukawa trees that had low horizontal branches that, along with some big boulders, made natural seating so that they could admire the jetty and how it looked with Jock's pretty boat tied up to it and the stunning backdrop of the water view and islands not too far away.

It was a perfect evening for a picnic too—a simple meal of sausages, grilled until their skins were crispy, wrapped in soft white bread with a liberal garnish of tomato sauce and a token lettuce leaf or two so that they could pretend it wasn't such an unhealthy meal. There was ginger beer for Jenni and lager with wedges of lime stuffed into the bottles for everyone else and there was the sound of animated conversation and frequent laughter and the feeling of...well, it felt more like family than friendship.

Dan hadn't felt like this in a group of people for so many years. Not since he'd walked away from the ruins of his marriage and members of his extended family, quite a few of whom had simply shaken their heads.

What did you expect, man? Get over it... She wanted kids and you weren't up to the job, were you?

The echo of the past was so faint it was more

than easy to ignore—it was just a part of some life baggage that no longer seemed nearly as important. He had moved on and life was so much better.

He raised the bottle of lager he was holding. 'Here's to *Lassie*,' he said. 'She's found her new home and I hope she remains here for many years to come.'

Jock and Grace exchanged a glance. And a look so full of love that Dan's breath caught in his chest.

'Like us…' Grace smiled.

'Just like us,' Jock agreed. His smile became his trademark cheeky grin. 'We've decided to get married,' he announced.

'That's old news,' Jenni said. 'You've been engaged for months.'

'No…we want to get *married*,' Grace said. 'Soon. Before you go home, Jen, so that you can be my bridesmaid. Will you…?'

Jenni had her hand pressed against her mouth. She looked as if she could start crying at any moment.

'Of course I will,' she said. 'I'd love to.'

Jock caught Dan's gaze and his grin faded to make his face unusually serious. 'I'm hoping you might be my best man,' he said.

Dan got why Jenni had looked so misty. He had a lump in his own throat now.

'Sure…' was the only response he managed, but

Jock didn't seem to mind. He was smiling again and he reached out to clink his bottle against Dan's.

'We only need two witnesses,' Grace added. 'And an approved celebrant. And we can get married anywhere we want to as long as we specify the place on our application.'

'What about here?' Jock suggested. 'On our own beach?'

'That would be perfect...' Grace leaned her head against Jock's shoulder. They were sharing that look again. The one that gave Dan the kind of poignant sensation that he recognised because he'd experienced it quite recently. When he'd been with Jenni at that ultrasound scan and he'd seen the baby's hand on the screen.

Yearning, that was what it was.

For things he'd believed he could never have.

Children.

Love.

A family of his own...

He had to make an effort to tune back into the conversation around him.

'So we submit the application and see a registrar to sign a statutory declaration that we're not already married, et cetera, pay a fee and have to wait three days and that's it. We could do late next week?'

Dan's jaw dropped. 'Next *week*?'

'It'll have to be soon.' Grace nodded. 'Jenni's

planning to go back to Scotland and the cut-off point for flying when you're pregnant is a lot sooner when you're carrying twins. She's only got a few weeks to play with here.'

Okay… Dan had known that his time with Jenni was only temporary. That she had every intention of returning to Scotland to have her babies, but…a couple of weeks? It felt like a ripple of sensation had just run down his spine and was now sending out tendrils of something cold and unpleasant. Had he really thought he had the chance of a future that included being a parent and a partner—to have a family of his own? How was that supposed to work when he would be living eighteen thousand kilometres away in an opposite time zone?

'Unless…'

Dan's voice sounded oddly raw. 'Unless what…?'

Grace glanced at Jenni, who shook her head firmly but it didn't stop her. 'I've been trying to persuade Jen that it might be a good idea for her to have the babies here in New Zealand,' she said. 'So that we could help out for the first few months, at least. She's got a year's maternity leave to play with, after all.'

This felt like a reprieve.

'Sounds like a good idea to me,' he said.

Grace and Jenni exchanged another glance that was very brief but seemed oddly significant. As if he'd said more than he realised? And then she looked back at Jock with her eyebrows raised as if she was encouraging him to say something.

Jock cleared his throat. 'We discovered something else when we were online finding out about the requirements for getting married in New Zealand,' he said. 'You don't have to be residents to get married here but we wanted to know how to go about applying for permanent residency and citizenship and we stumbled on something that we thought you should know about, Jen.'

'But I'm not going to emigrate,' Jenni said firmly. 'Scotland's home for me. You both *know* that.'

'Yes, but this isn't about you,' Jock said. 'Your children might want to live here one day. They're half Kiwis, after all.'

Dan closed his eyes for a heartbeat. Jock and Grace both believed he was the father of these babies.

Oh, man…he should have got on with it and had the repeat fertility test done long ago, shouldn't he? Jock was a medic. He'd be able to see those results and know just how likely it was that Jenni had to have made a mistake.

Why *hadn't* he got on with it?

He could have just excused himself by how busy he had been. Or how he might not want such a personal test being done in his place of work. But Dan knew it went a lot deeper than that. Maybe, on some level, he didn't want Jenni to know he wasn't the biological father of her babies because then she might not want to share the kinds of magic that Dan had never thought he could be part of. A scan to see the images of an unborn child. Permission to rest his hands on Jenni's belly to feel those babies moving with nothing more than a layer of skin between them.

And maybe…just maybe…there was that tiny hope that he could be wrong. That something might have changed. That perhaps, by some miracle, he really was the twins' father.

He didn't want to have to wake up from the dream just yet, that was what it was.

But he could hear the alarm sounding now. Loud and clear.

'We'll all be visiting as they grow up—especially if you and Jock are going to be here for ever,' Jenni added quietly. 'They can make their own choices about where to live when they're old enough.'

She looked disconcerted, Dan thought. Maybe she didn't want to think that far into the future. Or maybe she was regretting coming here to tell him that he was going to be a father and involving other people in decisions about her children's future.

It had been a brave thing to do, hadn't it?

But she had believed she was doing the right thing.

He felt proud of her for having that strength.

'But what we found out,' Jock said, 'was that if you have your babies in New Zealand and can prove that the father is a New Zealander, that makes them automatically citizens. They could hold two passports.'

Dan swallowed hard. Taking that fertility test had just become a priority. Along with a DNA test. They all had to know the truth. To see it there, in black and white on an official document.

'Does that not happen if they're not born in New Zealand?'

'They can apply but who knows? The rules might change by then.'

There was a moment's silence, broken by a sigh from Grace. 'Sorry… I didn't mean to spoil our picnic.' She looked as though she was pasting a smile onto her face. 'Where you have your babies is your decision, Jen. If you change your mind and stay for longer that will be fabulous, but we want to get married soon anyway. Don't we, Jock?'

'The sooner the better,' Jock agreed softly. He bent his head to plant a tender kiss on Grace's lips.

Dan found his own gaze seeking Jenni's and there it was, as if she'd already been looking at him. For a heartbeat, and then another, they held that gaze and it felt as if they were kissing each other with as much of a tender connection as Jock and Grace were enjoying.

He wanted, more than anything, to be alone with Jenni right now.

But that wasn't a good idea...because that would lead to physical intimacy, which made it so easy to ignore other things.

Important things, like the future.

And being completely honest with each other.

The moment was gone, in any case. Jock was getting to his feet.

'I'd better check *Lassie*'s moorings and get her secure for her first night in her new home.' He looked over his shoulder. 'Want to give me a hand, Dan?'

'Sure...'

Behind him, Grace and Jenni were starting to clear up the picnic leftovers and he could hear them talking about wedding plans.

Dan was making plans of his own. At the top of that list was to get a copy of his medical records and then to get on with repeating that test. But something else came a close second.

He wanted to talk to Jenni. To see if he might be able to persuade her to stay here to have the babies.

To give them more time to build the kind of trust that could provide a foundation for a future that Jenni might not have considered yet.

A future with *him*...

CHAPTER EIGHT

JENNI AND GRACE were both watching—and listening to—the drop in the baby's heart rate on the CTG machine.

As the contraction faded, the baby's heart rate increased again rapidly and then settled to a normal baseline rate. Jenni shared a glance with Grace, who was taking the lead in her first delivery since she'd started back at work part-time.

Both midwives had been in agreement that continuous CTG monitoring was a good idea when they'd noticed the variation of the baby's heart rate from intermittent monitoring as the first stage of labour progressed and it was reassuring that the baby was not showing any warning signs of distress, but Jules was getting tired. She'd been labouring for many hours overnight before Jenni and Grace had taken over her care when they came on duty at the hospital this morning. She was coping less well with the pain too, with only gas and air to help after a dose of intravenous analgesia had worn off some time ago. She reached for the mask Nathan was holding and jammed it against her face as each new contraction started.

Nathan was looking anxious. 'Is it normal for it to be taking this long?'

'Absolutely. Especially with a first baby.'

'I feel like I want to push,' Jules said.

'Let me check,' Grace told her. 'We don't want you to start pushing unless you're ready.'

There was a new energy in the room when Jules started pushing a short time later, leaning back against Nathan, putting her chin down on her chest to increase her efforts.

'You're doing it, Jules…' Nathan sounded as if he was imitating her pushing. 'Go, go, go…'

'Keep it going, Jules,' Grace encouraged. 'Keep pushing—as long as you can.'

Jules was giving it everything she had but, thirty minutes later, as the contractions continued relentlessly, Jenni looked up from the CTG screen to catch Grace's gaze.

'Variable decelerations,' she said, keeping her tone calm. She noted the W shape on the graph. 'And they're biphasic.'

'Shouldering?'

'No.' The spikes of a heart rate going high and then settling to a normal baseline again, known as 'shouldering', were absent. These were all signs of umbilical cord compression and a baby that was getting distressed through lack of oxygen.

'Can you give Jock a bell?'

Jenni stopped the printout of the screen and ripped off the trace. 'I'll be back in a minute.'

Jock's examination of Jules when he arrived was brief but thorough. 'Baby's getting tired,' he told Jules and Nathan. 'I think you're going to need some help.'

'I've changed my mind about having an epidural,' Jules said. 'But it's too late now, isn't it?'

'No. That's going to be our first step in helping to get your baby born as soon as possible.'

'Will I have to have a Caesarean?'

'That is an option,' Jock agreed, 'but we'll keep it up our sleeve for now. We have other things we can try first. Given where baby's head is now, the best option for you is for an assisted delivery—with forceps—as soon as your anaesthetic has taken effect.'

Jenni knew that Jock was also choosing forceps because it would be the fastest option to get this baby out safely. Given the changes they could see happening to the baby's condition, this could become a matter of life or death all too soon.

'I'm going to go over it all with you and Nathan and then we'll move you to Theatre,' Jock said. 'I can answer any more questions you have then, but I'd rather you were in the right place if it does become necessary for you to have a C-section.'

Both Grace and Jenni went to Theatre with Jules. It was Dan who was there to administer the spinal anaesthetic and, for just a very brief but rather unprofessional moment, Grace's glance was checking to see how pleased Jenni might be to see him.

And yes…the physical reaction to being this close to Daniel Walker—the way her heart rate picked up and that curl of sensation in her belly—was not something Jenni could control. Judging by the way Dan's gaze caught on hers for an instant longer than it needed to, it seemed that he was just as pleased to see her, which only intensified her reaction, but neither of them were about to let anything so personal interfere in any way with the job they were here to do.

The anaesthetic had taken effect by the time they had Nathan in his gown and mask and hat and Jock was scrubbed and ready for the instrumental delivery. Grace stood in position where she would be able to support Jules and coach her with her pushing and also to take the baby as soon as it was born if it wasn't in need of resuscitation. Jenni stood back, a little to one side of where Dan was at the head of the bed, monitoring Jules's vital signs. He could top up the drugs being administered for the spinal block if needed, or move to a general anaesthetic in the event of an emergency complication.

There was nothing for Jenni to do other than watch, which she was more than happy to do. Not just because she could steal the occasional peek at Dan as he worked but this was, in fact, the first time she'd seen her brother performing a forceps delivery and…she was impressed.

An episiotomy was needed to allow enough room to position the forceps correctly and then, between contractions, Jock gently slipped one handle into place for the curved blade to cradle one side of the baby's head. With the second handle positioned and the two locked together, they waited for the next contraction and for Jules to push as Jock applied pressure to pull.

'Here we go, Jules,' Grace told her. 'I know you can't feel it but bear down and push. Keep it going…'

'Good…' Jock was completely focused on his task. 'Try and get another push in for this contraction. We're almost there…'

'Oh…' Nathan was mesmerised by what he was seeing. 'I can see something,' he breathed. 'I can see her…what *is* that?'

'It's her hair.' It sounded like Jock was smiling beneath his mask. 'I'm going to take the forceps out now, Jules. You can push your baby out all by yourself with your next contraction.'

Which was exactly what Jules did. It wasn't the birth that Jenni was watching, though. She wasn't watching Jock any longer either. Because Dan was clearly as captivated as Nathan as he watched this baby girl being born and…watching *him* was making Jenni feel something new. An oddly intense but very real connection to this man. When you knew you were going to become a parent yourself in the very near future, it completely changed how it felt to witness a birth, didn't it?

It was even more intense for Jules and Nathan, of course. As Grace took the baby from Jock to put her skin to skin with Jules, both the young parents had tears streaming down their faces. When Nathan was given the task of cutting the umbilical cord the young couple shared a look of absolute pride—and wonder—with each other.

Grace looked after the delivery of the placenta and it was Jock who stitched up the episiotomy. Dan was continuing to monitor Jules as he shut off the anaesthetic and tidied up, but Jenni stayed where she was, blinking back a tear or two herself as she watched Nathan and Jules, blissfully un-aware of what was happening around them. They were both gazing at their newborn daughter, who lay quietly cradled in her mother's arms, clearly falling totally and utterly in love with the infant.

Jenni tried to swallow the lump in her throat as she shifted her gaze towards Dan. He was re-placing a bag of saline and adjusting the drip level to keep a vein open for Jules in case any other medication was needed so he didn't see her look-ing at him, but making eye contact wouldn't have changed anything. Jenni had made up her mind.

She couldn't do it.

She couldn't go back to the other side of the world and steal what was almost certainly the only opportunity Dan would ever have to be present at the birth of his own children. She couldn't steal the magic of these first minutes of being a parent and being able to experience this kind of falling in love that would be there for the rest of your life, no matter what.

It might be within her rights to do that.

But that didn't make it the right thing to do.

For a long, long moment Dan simply stood on the footpath without going through the gate to the old villa that was the hospital accommodation. He was staring at the steps to the veranda and thinking just how much his life had changed since he'd come here on the night of Jock's birthday to find Jenni sitting on those steps.

His life was about to change again—possibly not in a good way.

The dream was over.

Folded up in the back pocket of his jeans were the results from his semen analysis test. The results that could make Jenni realise she'd made a mistake. That she might need to search elsewhere to find the real father of her babies.

He took a deep breath and opened the gate but, just as he did so, the front door of the villa opened and Jenni came out. Her smile told him how pleased she was to see him and his heart sank a little bit further.

He loved that smile…

'Dan…just the person I need,' Jenni said. 'I've got Grace's car stuffed to the gills. Can you help me unload it, please?'

'Sure.' It was a relief to be able to put off the reason for his visit. 'What is it? Groceries?'

'No…baby stuff.' Jenni had reached the gate and she stood on tiptoes to give him a brief kiss. She was still smiling. 'Two bassinets. Two car seats. I found this online marketplace that sells all kinds of second-hand baby things.'

Dan blinked. And then he stared into the back hatch of Grace's car. Why on earth was Jenni buying ridiculously bulky items of baby gear when it would be far more practical to wait until she got back to Scotland before making such purchases?

He turned his head to find Jenni watching him. When she spoke, it felt like she was reading his mind as well.

'I'm not going back to Scotland,' she told him. 'Not yet, anyway. I'm going to stay here to have the babies.'

Dan simply stared at her. He could actually feel that folded piece of paper in his pocket, but how could he pull it out or even think of revealing its contents when Jenni was looking at him like *this*?

Did she have tears in her eyes?

'I can't do it, Dan.' Jenni spoke so softly it was little more than a whisper. 'I can't take away what could be the only chance you'll get to see your children being born. To see them take their

first breaths. To hold them in the first minutes
of their lives.'

Oh…*man*…

There was no way on earth that Dan could pull
that paper out of his pocket now. He opened his
mouth to say something but then simply closed
it again. He had no words…

Jenni didn't seem to mind. 'I can manage the
bassinets,' she said. 'But two car seats are quite
heavy. Could you carry those?'

Moving physically was a good thing. At least
his legs still knew what to do despite his brain
being mush.

'So I'm going to have the babies here and stay
for a few months,' Jenni told him. 'Grace was
right. It's a much better idea to have family around
to help for a while.'

Yeah…he remembered that conversation on the
beach. He'd thought it was a great idea that Jenni
stayed longer. To give them time to build a relationship that would mean he could live his dream
of having a family of his own. But what if those
results changed everything? Created another twist
in the story that took him further away from a
happy ending?

Maybe Jenni sensed that Dan needed some
time to get his head around this twist in the story
that the two of them were creating. Was that why
she was changing the subject?

'We're going shopping tomorrow,' she was saying. 'Getting up at the crack of dawn to get the early ferry, like we did the first time I was here and she took me sightseeing. This time we're going hunting for wedding things.' Her smile was even brighter than it had been when he'd arrived. 'It's going to be such fun.'

It also provided a means for Dan to escape before he ruined how happy Jenni was right now. He wouldn't stay, he said. She needed an early night because it was going to be a big day tomorrow.

He kissed her goodbye but he could still feel that folded paper in his pocket. So hot now if felt like it was burning his skin.

He knew he had to tell her.

He just couldn't do it right now.

'I'm so happy…'

'Of course you are. We're about to go shopping for your wedding dress.'

'I still think I could wear that dress I bought for your farewell party.'

Jenni laughed and patted her bump. 'I can't wear mine, that's for sure. And yes, that dress is very pretty but fuchsia pink doesn't exactly scream "bride", does it? You're only allowed to do this once—seeing as it's my brother you're getting married to.'

Grace gave a huff of laughter as if that warning was too ridiculous to merit a response. But then she tilted her head.

'We'd decided that all we needed was a simple family ceremony. No big deal, you know? I had no intention of screaming bride at all, but now...' Her smile wobbled a little. 'This is a big deal, isn't it? And I know it's the only time I'll ever want to do it. I think I *would* like to look like a bride and have flowers and fairy lights, maybe even a garter.'

'*Yes*...' Jenni was nodding enthusiastically. 'Let's do this properly. Those bridal boutiques won't know what's hit them. This is going to be so much fun...'

Jenni and Grace were at the back of the inter-island ferry, leaning over the rail, captivated by the stunning scenery of the Sounds they were sailing through as the sun rose. They were also hoping they might be a bit luckier than last time and get to spot a pod of dolphins.

'It's not just that I'm getting married,' Grace said then. 'I'm this happy that you've decided to have the babies here. Can I be your midwife?'

'Yes. But Jock can't be my obstetrician, even if something happens so that Maria can't be there. I'm not having my brother looking at bits of me I haven't even seen myself.'

Grace laughed. 'Fair enough.'

Jenni let her breath out in a sigh. 'Do you remember what we were talking about the last time we did this?'

'About your mother?' Grace sounded serious

now. 'And how you and Jock never felt like you had a proper home?'

'Aye… I was worried that Jock was never going to stay in one place long enough to put down roots and he'd never feel like he had a real home and he'd never be truly happy.' She stopped for a moment and then threw her arms around Grace. 'I can't believe I'm so lucky that I'm going to get my best friend as my sister-in-law. And I've never seen Jock this happy. Ever. He adores you.'

'I feel the same way about him.' But Grace wriggled free of the embrace. 'We'll both be bawling our eyes out in a minute if we keep this up. Let's talk about something else. Have you heard back from the friend that's renting your house in Glasgow?'

'Yes. And she's more than happy to stay there for as long as she can, so her rent will cover what I'll be paying for somewhere here.'

'It's a shame you can't stay in the hospital accommodation.'

'I won't be a hospital employee by then. You'll be back full-time. Besides, it would hardly be fair to be keeping any new staff members awake all night with crying babies.'

'You know you can stay with us. We won't mind being kept awake.'

'Be good practice for the future, I guess.' Jenni smiled. 'But no… I really do need my own place. I'm going to have to learn to manage by myself before I head home. Not that it won't be fabulous to have you and Jock on hand to rescue me to start with.'

'And Dan…'

'Aye…and Dan…'

'Have you told him yet? That the babies are going to be born in New Zealand?'

'Only last night. I've hardly seen him in the last few days. He came around when I got back from collecting that second-hand baby gear I found online. It was fairly obvious I wasn't going to be putting things like bassinets and car seats in my suitcase to go home.'

'What did he say when he knew you were staying?'

'He went a bit quiet, to be honest.' Jenni bit her lip. She really wasn't that sure how thrilled Dan had been at her news.

He hadn't even stayed to have a meal with her, saying that Jenni needed to get up so early to catch the ferry that he didn't want her to lose any more sleep.

He had kissed her, but even that had felt…different? As if his mind was somewhere else entirely.

'It must be overwhelming,' Grace said. 'Being present at the birth is a pretty emotional thing.' She hesitated for a beat. 'Will you let him be there the whole time?'

'Yes… If that's what he wants. That was the

main reason I decided to stay here. I didn't think it would be fair to take away an experience he might never get the chance to have, otherwise.'

Grace nodded. 'It's all about bonding, isn't it? And that's going to underpin his involvement with the twins for the rest of his life.'

And with her for the rest of *her* life...?

Okay, maybe it wasn't surprising that he'd needed some space to get used to the idea. This was huge. Not as life-changing as becoming a mother, but it was still huge.

It wasn't something Jenni had ever planned— to have a particular man as a significant part of her life. It should be a disturbing concept but... this was Dan, wasn't it?

He was a friend.

More than a friend. She couldn't say they were lovers because she wasn't *in* love with Dan and this physical relationship was only ever going to be temporary—maybe it was already fading, in fact—but...she cared about him.

As a friend.

As the father of her children.

And that was definitely a form of love.

So...aye...she loved Daniel Walker.

The swift mental gymnastics that had allowed this conclusion to surface with such conviction hadn't changed anything.

This still felt safe.

It still felt that she had done the right thing to

come here and tell Dan the truth face to face. It didn't feel dangerous that they had become a lot closer than either of them might have predicted and it didn't feel like a mistake to have made the decision to stay a few months longer.

It wasn't going to change the big picture. She and Dan were totally on the same page. He was just as happy as she was to stay away from a committed relationship with a partner. It wasn't as if they were planning to get married. Or even live in the same country in the near future. It would, however, make their connection as co-parents stronger and that had to be a good thing.

They could remain the best of friends for the rest of their lives. They could love and care about each other as well as loving and caring for the children they shared. It could possibly work better than most marriages, in fact.

It would definitely work better than any of her mother's marriages or relationships, that was for sure.

'Hey...' Grace broke into her thoughts. 'You never told me what the results were of that fertility test Dan was going to get done?'

'I don't know myself. I don't think the results have come back yet.'

'But he did that test well over a week ago, didn't he? Right after that night when we were talking about how it would be a good idea for the twins to be born here.'

'A few days later. He had to…you know…abstain from sex for at least three days.'

'Oh…guess it might take a bit longer, then.'

'Mmm…' Jenni tried to make it sound unimportant but that abstinence hadn't been broken yet, had it? Was that why she was starting to think the attraction might be wearing off? Maybe Dan had actually come around the other night to tell her it was over and, if it was, she would be okay with that.

But was it a coincidence that the last time they'd made love had been before the night of the beach picnic? When they'd talked about the potential rights of the twins to become New Zealand citizens.

Jenni could feel herself frowning and deliberately pushed away whatever doubts were trying to sneak up on her. This was going to be a happy day that she and Grace would be able to remember for ever. They were going to shop till they dropped for dresses and other bridal necessities like flowers to wear in their hair and possibly a veil and garter and pretty underwear for Grace. They would be more than ready for a late lunch and then a dash back to catch the ferry home. And there were so many other things to talk about. Even though this was going to be a very small and simple ceremony, there was still a lot of planning and organisation to be done and that had to be Jenni's priority for the next couple of days.

If banishing doubts about how Dan had reacted to knowing he could be present at the birth of his children was going to contribute to making this special day as perfect as possible for both her best friend and her brother, then that was exactly what Jenni was going to do.

She wasn't about to let anything spoil such a special day.

'Oh, *look*, Grace…' Jenni pointed at the splash she had just seen not far from the ship. Graceful grey shapes could be seen taking turns to arc over the calm water and then dive to speed through the sea, still visible just under the surface. *'Dolphins…'*

She could feel her smile stretching right across her face.

This was a sign, wasn't it?

This wedding *was* going to be perfect.

It was about as perfect as it could be, Dan decided.

The autumn weather was lovely, warm enough for the summery kind of dresses both Grace and Jenni were wearing, and there was not a breath of wind. The tree-covered islands in the distance, a fishing boat that was anchored not far out from the beach and even the jetty and *Lassie* were being perfectly reflected in the mirror-calm surface of the clear, dark sea water.

It was too light for the fairy lights that had been strung in the Pohutukawa trees overhanging the beach but they would come into their own later, when a few close friends had been invited to join them all on the beach for an epic evening barbecue. This part of the day, however, was intimate. Right now, the only people standing in silence broken occasionally by birdsong were himself, an uncharacteristically nervous-looking Jock and the celebrant, a local woman called Aroha who might be well into her sixties but her delight in her job hadn't dimmed. She knew how to use technology too, and had the music that had been chosen loaded onto her phone, which was connected to a Bluetooth speaker hidden between rocks.

At the appointed time she started the music that was Grace's cue to come down the path to the beach, so he was listening to John Legend's romantic song when he saw Jenni for the first time in days.

Since the evening when she'd told him about her decision to stay here to give birth.

When she'd invited him to be present at the birth of the children she was so confident were his.

The same day he'd received the semen analysis test results that confirmed just how impossible that was, because the figures were even worse than they had been when he'd been tested the first time.

He'd gone to see her to show her the report because she needed to know the truth. Good grief...

she had decided to stay here for the twins' birth after that conversation with Jock and Grace about them having automatic citizenship if they were born in their father's country. They all thought his name was going to be recorded on their birth certificates. They all needed to know the truth.

But then Jenni had blindsided him with her invitation to include him in the birth and early months of the twins' lives—and that was another layer to the fantasy of parenthood that he had been allowing himself to indulge in ever since he'd been present at that scan.

It was going too far, though, being present at something as intimate as the birth if he wasn't the biological father. If Jenni still wanted him to be there when she knew the truth then he would embrace the experience, but it could only happen on a foundation of honesty and he just hadn't been able to find the right words that night.

And then she'd been away with Grace to go shopping in Wellington, work had been frantically busy yesterday and she'd disappeared with Grace today to go to a hairdresser and florist and then hide themselves in the house to get ready. Not that he could say anything today, of course. This was Jock and Grace's day, and the expression on his best mate's face as he watched the woman he loved walk onto the beach brought a lump to Dan's throat.

The bride walked between the boulders onto

the small sandy beach and…she looked stunning. Her lacy dress wasn't blindingly white—more of an ivory shade. The top fitted her like a glove but the skirt swirled with every step. She had tiny daisy-like flowers woven into her long blonde hair that was hanging in loose waves and she carried a simple bouquet of long-stemmed blooms that matched the ones in her hair.

No wonder Jock was looking like all his dreams were coming true. Grace was looking at him in exactly the same way and the love between these two people was enough to light up the whole beach. That lump in Dan's throat suddenly grew jagged edges.

This was what was missing from his own life.

And always would be…

Oh, help… Dan had to make sure that the shaft of pain—and loss—he was feeling wasn't showing on his face during this happiest of occasions. He shifted his gaze from the bride and, just as the song was soaring into its chorus about all of him loving all of her, he saw Jenni come through the boulders and onto the sand.

For Dan, she looked even more stunning than the bride.

Jenni was wearing a dress in a shade of bluey green that looked like sea water. It fitted snugly over her breasts and there was a knot beneath them in the centre of the dress that cleverly allowed for extra fabric to fall elegantly over the bump of her belly. Her arms were bare and her hair was also loose—fiery auburn waves that were catching the last of the day's sunlight.

She was smiling. Of course she was. Her best friend was getting married to her brother and she couldn't be happier about it. Except that it wasn't Jock or Grace that she was smiling at.

It was him.

As he held her gaze and smiled back, Dan could feel something in his chest that he'd thought he would never feel again. A feeling of warmth and softness that was expanding at a rate that threatened to break something.

Like his heart…?

It was love, that was what it was. Maybe it was an echo of the energy that Jock and Grace were creating.

Or maybe Dan had just woken up to the fact that he was in this a whole lot deeper than he'd realised.

He had fallen in love with Jenni McKay.

Jenni had to wipe tears away more than once during the ceremony.

Jock and Grace had written their vows themselves and it felt like she and Dan were privileged to be included in something that was a very private part of the love between them.

They held both of each other's hands as they

stood in front of the celebrant, with Dan and Jenni on either side.

Grace had spoken first. 'We're all searching for a place to call home,' she said softly. 'But we both know now that home is bigger than just a place. That it might not *be* a place at all. That it might be a person...' She had to catch her breath and brush away a tear. 'Because home *is* where the heart is. You're my home, Jock McKay. You're my heart. I will love you for as long as I live...'

Jock had cleared his throat, blinked back tears and then taken a deep breath. 'When otters are sleeping they hold hands so they don't float away from each other. We did that once in the sea, not very far from where we are right now. I held your hand and you held mine and...and that's what I will always do for you, Grace Collins, because I love you and always will. It doesn't matter whether I'm actually touching you or not, I'll be holding your hand—so you don't float away...'

Oh, *my*... The tears were gathering yet again. Enough to make Jenni's vision more than slightly blurry even after a couple had escaped. Had it been the way she'd touched her face to brush them away that had caught Dan's attention? Was that why she could feel the intensity of the way he was looking at her? She couldn't stop her gaze slipping sideways to catch his. Was it the blurriness that made it seem like he was looking at her as if he didn't want *her* to float away?

As if…

As if he loved her?

As if he was *in* love with her?

Was it contagious? Weddings were notorious for making guests realise how they felt about life and love and each other. Was that what was happening here?

Did Jenni want it to be what was happening?

Jock and Grace were exchanging their formal vows now and Jenni could feel the words resonating as if she was speaking them herself.

I do…

CHAPTER NINE

THAT FEELING—that glow of hope and longing and a kind of joy she'd never felt before—stayed with Jenni for the rest of that magical day when her beloved twin brother got married to her best friend.

It was still there the next day and the day after that, and that was when she began to wonder if it was more than simply an echo of the wedding joy she'd been immersed in. If it could possibly be…*real*…?

Not that she'd had the chance to spend any time with Dan after the wedding. With a run of split shifts to cover, he seemed as absent from work as Grace and Jock, who had taken some annual leave to fly down to Queenstown for a brief honeymoon. Without Grace, Jenni was kept busier at work, which was getting more and more tiring, but she was busy out of work hours too. New staff members were due to move into the hospital accommodation, which was the push Jenni needed to make a serious effort to find her own house to rent in Picton.

She was online as soon as she got home, searching for any new rental properties that had become available, preferably immediately available. She wanted to move as soon as possible so that she could stop working in a week or two and put all her energy into getting ready for the birth of her babies.

Nesting…

It was something Jenny had imagined doing ever since she knew she was pregnant. She could see bassinets made up with snowy white sheets and soft blankets with colourful mobiles hanging over them. A baby's bath and piles of nappies. Tiny clothes neatly stacked on shelves and cute cuddly toys on a windowsill waiting for their turn to be useful. She'd just never imagined she would be doing it on this side of the world.

But being displaced wasn't as daunting as it could have been, thanks to Jock and Grace's wedding. Echoes of the vows they had exchanged had stayed with Jenni as strongly as that feeling of wanting Dan as an integral part of her future.

The idea that *home* could come in the shape of a person rather than a place.

Could love really be trusted that much? Could it be as solid as the ground beneath your feet and the walls and roof of a house to shelter you?

Her brother—who'd grown up with exactly the same reasons not to trust the people who claimed to love you—was prepared to believe it was. Enough to let him risk giving his heart to someone.

Jenni wanted to believe it was but...it would be the biggest step she had ever taken.

Because if she could believe it, she might— finally—be able to let go of what she'd believed with such certainty all her life—that you couldn't trust everybody to be telling the truth and that offering someone else your heart was quite likely to be the fastest road to broken dreams and a miserable life.

But now there was that glow that wasn't fading into oblivion and perhaps it was a good thing that she hadn't seen Dan since the wedding because it wouldn't take much for it to be snuffed out. She would only need to see something in his face or hear a note in his tone that tickled one of those doubts she'd managed to bury and she'd be running, wouldn't she?

She might remember the way he'd reacted when she'd told him she was going to stay for the birth of the twins. Or that the last time he'd held her or had his hands on her belly to wait for the movement of the babies had been the night of the picnic, when Jock and Grace had shared their plans to get married. Now they were away on their honeymoon, so it had been...oh, *help*...more than two weeks ago?

The reminder of Jock and Grace being away was timely. Jenni shut her laptop and hauled herself to her feet. She had promised to go and water Grace's indoor pot plants while she was away and she'd completely forgotten about it until now. Going out again was the last thing her sore feet and tired body would have chosen after a long day at work, but how guilty would she feel if they came back to find their plants dying? And, on the bright side, she could pick up a takeaway on the way back and that would save her having to cook anything for her dinner.

There was an even brighter side that was totally unexpected. Having watered the plants and locked the front door of the house behind her, Jenni was startled to find Dan arriving.

'I promised Jock I'd look in and check on *Lassie*,' he said.

'I've just been watering the plants.' Jenni could feel her heart beating against her ribs. She was searching Dan's face for signs that the surprise of finding her here might not be a pleasant one but she couldn't see any.

He was smiling.

There was a softness in his face and in those gorgeous brown eyes that reminded her of the way he'd been looking at her during that emotional moment of the vows that Jock and Grace had been making to each other.

And if her brain was still trying to come up with a reason not to trust what she thought she was seeing, it was silenced completely as Dan stepped closer.

Close enough to touch her face. To let his hand slip behind her neck and then let his fingers thread themselves into her hair to cradle the back of her head.

To kiss her.

Slowly.

Tenderly.

In a way that made that glow become so bright that, even though Jenni had her eyes firmly closed, it felt bright enough to blind her.

'It feels like ages since I've seen you,' Dan said softly when he finally raised his head. 'I've missed you, Jen.'

'Mmm…' Jenni felt completely out of breath. 'Same…'

'Come down to the beach with me while I check *Lassie*'s moorings? Then, maybe I could take you out to dinner? I'm doing a night shift tonight and I don't have to be at work until ten p.m.'

Miraculously, Jenni's fatigue seemed to be evaporating. 'Sounds wonderful,' she said.

Dan took her hand as they reached the steps that led down to the beach and he didn't let go even when they reached the safety of soft, flat sand. They walked through the boulders to have that beautiful backdrop to the wedding in front of them again. Jenni could feel the warmth of Dan's hand holding hers and could hear the echo of Jock's oh, so loving words to Grace about being her otter and always holding her hand so she wouldn't float away and…

And she knew *she* could trust *this*.

She could feel Dan's gaze resting on her and she looked up, knowing that making eye contact with him would make this absolutely real.

And it did.

'I love you, Jenni,' Dan said—so softly his words were no more than a whisper.

'I love you too,' Jenni whispered back.

'I never thought I'd ever feel like this again. Or be able to trust it.'

Jenni's nod was almost shy. 'Same…'

'I want to be with you for the twins' birth. I want to be a part of their lives—a part of *your* life, Jenni McKay.' She could hear the way Dan sucked in a deep breath.

Okay…that glow was definitely blinding now. So bright it was painful. It was more like the light of an explosion than something warm and comfortable. Was it too much, too soon?

Dan was still talking. Jenni forced herself to focus. Had he just said *'But'*…?

'It wouldn't make any difference at all. I'll love the twins as if they *were* my own children.'

Wait…

What…?

Jenni felt her body moving backwards as if Dan had just forcefully pushed her away from him.

She took another step more slowly and then sank onto one of the larger boulders because it didn't feel as if her legs wanted to hold her upright any longer.

'What did you just say?' Her words emerged sounding bewildered, as if she couldn't possibly have heard him correctly.

'That I want us to live together.' Dan's tone had changed as well. There was a puzzled note in it. 'To be a family…'

'A family with children that you don't believe are yours?'

'They can't be.' Dan crouched in front of the boulder Jenni was sitting on, so that his face was closer to hers. 'I'm really sorry…but the odds of that being the case are astronomically small. My test results are worse than they were when I first got tested more than ten years ago.'

It sounded as if Dan's voice was coming from much further away than it was.

'In a healthy male there should be twenty million sperm in every millilitre of semen. Mine doesn't even crack one million. And yeah…it does only take one sperm, but with numbers like that the only way it has even a remote chance of being successful is for it to be injected directly into an egg. Intracytoplasmic technology.'

His voice was clearer now. The shock of what he'd said was finally wearing off. What was taking its place was a disappointment that was so bitter it instantly morphed into overwhelming anger.

Jenni's voice was even clearer than Dan's. And much, much colder. As cold as ice.

'I asked you whether you still thought I was lying and you said "no". I *believed* you.'

It had been the moment that changed everything, hadn't it? The memory of that intimate connection they'd discovered with each other had grown and pulled them back together with a force she'd never known could exist between two people. Her breath came out in an incredulous huff of sound.

'It was enough to persuade me to trust you enough to have *sex* with you again, for God's sake. And now you're saying I *was* lying all along?'

'No…' Dan's hand covered one of Jenni's that was lying protectively on the top of her bump. 'I did say I didn't think you were lying because I knew *you* believed you weren't lying. It's just a mistake, that's all. There's a window of time on either side of an estimated conception date. You were on holiday…'

His voice trailed off, as if he realised that what he was suggesting was humiliating. To be fair, he only had his own experience to have based his reasoning on.

'So…what you're really saying is that I spent my holiday having one-night stands with any man

I met along the way?' She pulled her hand out from beneath Dan's.

He stood up again and used that hand to rub his forehead. 'No,' he said. 'That's not what I'm suggesting at all. But you did go from here to visit your old boyfriend in Melbourne, didn't you?'

'Jeremy.' Jenni's voice was still icy. 'Who's now married. Happily married. With kids.' She pushed herself to her feet. 'So, no… I didn't jump into bed with him for old time's sake.'

She turned towards the path and steps that led back to the house. And to where she'd parked Grace's car. She had to escape.

Now…

'This was never going to work,' she said, without looking at Dan. 'I thought I was doing the right thing, but it's clearly been the biggest mistake I've ever made and there's no point in dragging this out any longer. Hopefully, it's not too late to change my arrangements and get on the first plane I can back to Scotland.' She lifted her chin and turned her head just far enough to catch his gaze. 'I don't want you in my life, Daniel Walker.'

Jenni started walking away. 'I don't want you in the lives of my children either.'

CHAPTER TEN

OBSTETRIC CONSULTANT MARIA GOULD looked up from the report she was reading and the expression on her face made Jenni McKay's heart skip a beat.

'There's something wrong, isn't there? Something that showed up on the biophysical profile ultrasound?' Jenni found she was holding her breath.

She had taken the test yesterday afternoon, where sensors had been strapped to her belly to record the heart rates of each twin and individual ultrasounds done to measure and score their body movements, muscle tone, breathing movements and the amount of amniotic fluid around them.

She had not invited Dan to attend the appointment.

Despite her best efforts, however, she'd thought about him the whole time it was happening but she had refused to let herself feel guilty. He didn't believe these twins were his babies. He didn't deserve to be there.

He had tried to call her more than once after she'd walked out on him the night before last. She hadn't picked up and then she had blocked his number. When she'd seen him at a distance at work yesterday, she'd turned and walked in the other direction without making eye contact. Luckily, no one in her care had been in need of any kind of anaesthetic.

Jenni was still angry.

Deeply disappointed.

Hurt beyond measure.

She didn't want to talk to the man who only believed she wasn't lying to him because he believed that she'd been having sex with other men. Besides, she'd been ridiculously busy, both at work and at home. She had handed in her resignation to take effect almost immediately—as soon as Grace got back from her honeymoon in a day or two and could take back her caseload. She'd made the appointment with Maria and persuaded Mandy to fit her in for the extra ultrasound test. She'd pored over flight itineraries, booked and paid for airline tickets. She'd started packing...

Jenni couldn't let go of that breath that had caught deep in her chest until Maria smiled. 'Nothing wrong showed up on the profile,' she said. 'Quite the contrary. The twins both scored nine—normal is eight to ten. They're a good weight. Twin A is one point two kilos and Twin B is one point four. That's about three pounds and three point two pounds. I'm happy to stay with the estimated delivery date we came up with originally, but that means you're getting close to thirty-two weeks.'

Jenni nodded, pulling in a new, deeper breath with relief.

'You're pushing it.' Maria's tone was worried. 'For international travel.' She picked up another piece of paper from her desk. 'You're planning to fly from Blenheim to Auckland, connect with an international flight to London via Singapore and then take a domestic flight from London to Glasgow. Total travel time of nearly *thirty-five* hours?'

Jenni bit her lip. 'I know…it's horrible.'

'The airline requires a clearance from me. I have to sign my name to information about this being a multiple pregnancy, whether there are any complications, the EDD and whether I think you're fit to travel.'

'I am fit to travel,' Jenni assured her. 'And I haven't crossed the thirty-two-week barrier yet.'

'That could well be debated. Especially if any-thing went wrong—like delivering premature twins at thirty thousand feet. Or a pilot having to divert the plane to get you to a hospital. Have you got travel insurance?'

'That needs a clearance from you as well,' Jenni admitted. 'I *have* to travel…' She could feel her eyes filling with tears. 'It's…to do with the babies' father,' she added, her voice cracking. 'I have to get back home and if I don't go now it'll be too late...'

Too late for her to escape, but she couldn't tell Maria that. Jenni might prefer to never have to see Daniel Walker again in her life but she still wasn't going to risk making his involvement in her pregnancy public. One day, in a future so far away she didn't need to think about it right now, her children might want to find their biological father. It would be best if he was prepared to make that easy and that would be a lot less likely if he'd been subjected to widespread judgement or disapproval of the way he had denied paternity. He was probably going to get enough shade from Jock and Grace anyway, when they found out what was going on.

Maria had made the assumption, at her first appointment, that the twins' father lived in Scotland. Now she was probably thinking that her relationship was in jeopardy or that her partner was desperately ill. She certainly looked torn.

'How are *you* feeling?' she queried. 'Be honest, please...'

'I'm a bit short of breath sometimes,' Jenni responded. 'I get some backache, I need to pee frequently, and I'm not sleeping that well. The usual stuff for this stage of pregnancy. Better than usual for a multiple pregnancy.'

Any physical symptoms were compounded

by feeling more utterly miserable than she had ever felt in her life, of course, but she couldn't tell Maria that either. She had to be strong. This was about her future. And the future of her children. They deserved to grow up with a mother who respected herself enough to know that she couldn't be with someone who didn't believe in her integrity.

Maria was silent for a long moment and then she sighed as she picked up her pen. 'Okay... I'll sign you off, but you've still got forty-eight hours before your first flight. If *anything* changes, I want to know about it.'

Jenni nodded. 'I won't go anywhere if I think there's any danger to these babies,' she said quietly. 'They're my absolute priority.'

'Are you working today?'

'It's my last full day. I'll be tying up loose ends tomorrow, ready to hand everything back to Grace.' Jenni got to her feet. 'I might even get most of that done today.'

'Don't tempt fate,' Maria warned but she was smiling. 'Best of luck.' She handed over the sheet of paper that was her clearance for Jenni to travel. 'It's been a pleasure meeting you.' She raised an eyebrow. 'Does Jock know that you're rushing back to Scotland?'

'Not yet. I didn't want to tell him while he's on his honeymoon.' Jenni folded the paper carefully, trying—and failing—to squash another pang of guilt. 'Thanks so much for all your help, Maria.'

Jenni remembered Maria's warning about tempting fate the moment she walked back to the maternity ward to find that Lynn Grimshaw had arrived with her partner, Chris. She was in established labour, with strong, regular contractions and already five centimetres dilated.

She remembered it again several hours later, when she had to call for the obstetrician on duty—who happened to be Maria—when the labour had failed to progress despite trying everything Jenni suggested, like walking around, changing positions, bouncing on a birth ball, a hot shower... Lynn was getting tired, her contractions were getting weaker and there were some decelerations happening with the baby's heart rate. A decision was made to start an oxytocin infusion to augment labour, to do a bedside ultrasound to check the position of the foetal head in relation to the pelvis and Lynn asked to have an epidural as well.

Fate—having been tempted—apparently had one last ace up her sleeve when it came to the anaesthetist on duty because it was Daniel Walker who walked into the room a short time later as Mandy was doing the ultrasound examination.

For a horrible moment Jenni actually wondered if she could do this. If she could be totally professional and not let anything to do with her personal life affect her professional abilities. Emotions were threatening to overwhelm her. The anger was still there but the hurt was far more powerful.

Thank goodness Maria had stayed to observe the ultrasound and the initial effects of the infusion. She introduced Dan to their patient and her partner and gave him all the medical information he needed and that gave Jenni a good couple of minutes to centre herself and get into a space where nothing personal could interfere in any way with her part in something that was a critical time in the life of both a mother and a baby.

This was her last day at work here.

The last time she would ever have to be in the room with the man who'd broken her heart so badly.

She could do this.

She *had* to be able to do this...

Good grief...she looked so pale...

Unwell, even.

And it was his fault, wasn't it?

For the space of a heartbeat and then another, Dan actually wondered if he could be in this room and give a hundred percent to the woman who needed his medical care.

Maria was filling him in. 'Lynn Grimshaw is a thirty-eight-year-old primigravida, full-term, textbook pregnancy with no known issues. Foetal lie is longitudinal with a cephalic presentation.'

Dan nodded but it was an effort to focus. If he

couldn't…if too much of his mind—and heart—were on the care that another woman in this room needed—the woman he loved, he would have to excuse himself somehow from this patient and find someone else to administer this epidural anaesthetic.

'Lynn went into spontaneous labour fourteen hours ago. She came in this morning at five centimetres dilated but has failed to progress past six centimetres for more than four hours. Decelerations of the foetal heart rate have been noted so we started an oxytocin infusion nearly an hour ago. Contraction strength has improved and she's currently at seven centimetres dilated.'

Maybe it was the way Dan saw Jenni's shoulders move, as if she was straightening her back to face whatever she had to deal with, that suddenly brought everything into sharp focus for himself.

This wasn't about them. It was about a tired mother, her anxious partner and a baby that was in increasingly urgent need of a safe arrival. Jenni was handling this like a professional and so could he.

He picked up Lynn's chart and noted the last vital sign recordings. 'She tachycardic,' he murmured. 'Heart rate of one fifteen. Her blood pressure's a bit low at ninety-six over fifty-five.' He looked at the screen of the ultrasound machine and lowered his voice. 'There's no indications of placental abruption or bleeding, is there?'

'No, but the sensitivity for picking it up on ultrasound can be as low as twenty-five percent.
There's no visible bleeding.' Maria was also looking at the screen. 'I'm happy with the foetal head
position too, if we need to go for an instrumental delivery.'

'The sooner we get the epidural in the better,
then.' Dan stepped towards Lynn. 'I'm going to
get you to sit with your legs over the edge of the
bed,' he told her. 'Jenni will help you lean forward and stay as still as possible. This won't take
long…'

Fifteen minutes later, the epidural had taken
full effect but the pain relief hadn't reduced
Lynn's rapid heart rate or breathing. Dan made
the decision to stay in the room a while longer.
It was probably because Jenni was here that the
atmosphere felt so tense but instinct was telling
him that something else was contributing to this
feeling of unease. Lynn was his patient now as
well. He wasn't going to leave until he was confident there was nothing to worry about.

Was Jenni feeling that frisson of concern too?
Or was she concentrating on the screen of the
CTG machine in order to avoid catching his gaze?

'You're doing well,' Jenni told Lynn. 'Your contractions are still strong and they're lasting well.'

'I feel weird.' Lynn reached for her partner's
hand. 'Something's wrong, Chris…'

Maria straightened up from doing an internal

examination. 'You're in transition, Lynn,' she said. 'That can make you feel anxious. You're at least eight centimetres now. You'll be able to start pushing very soon.'

'No...' Lynn's head rolled from side to side on her pillow. 'I feel...sick...'

'That's normal,' Jenni assured her, but her gaze flicked past Dan and he could feel something change in the room again.

Concern was growing...

'What's happening...?' Lynn sounded frightened now.

'Your waters have finally broken,' Jenni responded. 'It's okay, Lynn...'

Except it wasn't. Dan could see that the fluid had a green stain that meant it contained meconium.

'I want to get up,' Lynn said. 'Please... Chris... I have to go home...'

Chris looked at Jenni, his eyes wide with alarm.

'It hurts,' Lynn cried.

'What hurts?' Dan's heart rate picked up. Was the epidural infusion failing?

'My chest...' Lynn was gasping now. 'I can't breathe...' She fell back against her pillows.

'Foetal heart rate's dropping,' Jenni warned as an alarm sounded on the CTG machine.

Maria was moving fast. 'She's fully dilated,' she said moments later, turning to her registrar.

'Open that forceps kit for me, please. We need to get this baby out.'

'Lynn…?' Dan was at the head of the bed. He gripped her shoulder. 'Can you hear me? Open your eyes…'

Dan was removing the pillows from behind Lynn so that he could tilt her head back and open her airway.

Because she wasn't breathing…

He had to ask Chris to step back so that he could get to the bag mask and put it over Lynn's face to help her breathe.

'Sorry, mate…we need a bit of space…'

But Chris wasn't moving. He was standing, stunned, as though he couldn't understand what was happening. Jenni moved swiftly and took hold of his arm.

'Come over here, Chris. Look…your baby's being born…'

She had to leave Chris standing by himself seconds later, as a limp-looking baby emerged and was put into the towel Jenni grabbed. The registrar headed for the phone, presumably to summon the assistance of neonatal paediatrics. Maria was dealing with what looked like a significant post-partum haemorrhage and Dan…

Dan couldn't find a pulse.

'Someone push the cardiac arrest button,' he shouted. 'I'm starting CPR.'

* * *

Dear *Lord*...

Jenni had to think faster and focus harder than she ever had or she might have become as frozen as poor Chris was right now. She'd stand there watching the controlled chaos of the response to an emergency situation and listen to directions being called and alarms sounding and all she'd be thinking about was how could this have gone so horribly wrong?

At least she had something to do that needed all her concentration. This baby girl was scarily pale and limp. Jenni put her down on the waterproof mattress of the resuscitation table, beneath the radiant heat source. Using a soft towel, she began drying the baby with firm stroking movements—on her head, her body and her legs to provide stimulation as well as removing the moisture that would be sucking away body heat. She looked up as she wrapped another dry towel around the infant to see the registrar standing, hands poised above Lynn's chest to restart the chest compressions as soon as she was intubated. Maria was doing bimanual compression, clearly trying to control the amount of blood Lynn was losing. Dan was bent over Lynn's head, his concentration fierce enough to be palpable. He had a laryngoscope blade in her mouth and was slipping an endotracheal tube into place to secure her airway for ventilation.

MIRACLE TWINS TO HEAL THEM

The baby was gasping rather than breathing well herself so Jenni positioned her head to open her airway before she placed the disc of a stethoscope on the small chest. The heart rate was less than a hundred—too slow. She picked up one of the small, round masks to check that it was the right size to make a good seal over the tiny mouth and nose. Then she attached it to an Ambu bag and gave five slow, gentle breaths, watching the small chest to make sure the lungs were being inflated.

The baby's colour was improving. Jenni was about to recheck the heart rate when the first of the extra medical teams summoned burst into the room. The cardiac arrest crew on call surrounded the bed but somehow, a few seconds later, Dan slipped through the tight group of people to appear beside the resuscitation table. He caught Jenni's gaze.

'What can I do?'

It was only then that Jenni realised how alone she'd been, looking after this newborn. How *scared* she'd been...

And that tone in Dan's voice. The focus. The offer of support. The caring... It was enough to bring the prickle of tears to the back of Jenni's eyes. But it was the baby who began to cry. She was getting rapidly pinker too, and starting to move her arms and legs.

'I think we're okay,' Jenni told Dan. She caught his gaze again for a heartbeat. 'But…thank you.'

She picked up the baby girl and took her to Chris, who was still standing to one side. His view of what was being done to help Lynn was almost totally obstructed by so many people but that was probably a good thing because, from what Jenni could hear, the resuscitation was not going well.

Chris began crying as he saw the baby. Silently, with the tears rolling unchecked down his face. His hands were shaking as he reached out to touch her.

'Is she okay…?'

'She's good. She needed a wee bit of help, but now she's doing well.'

'Can I hold her?' Chris asked, his voice breaking. 'Please…?'

He needed something to hold onto, didn't he? As the world as he knew it was apparently disintegrating.

'Come and sit down,' Jenni said gently, her heart breaking for him. 'I think being held by her daddy is exactly what your daughter needs.'

What both father and baby needed.

The paediatric team arrived but didn't immediately take the baby from her father's arms. Bags of blood and IV fluids were being delivered. More and different drugs were being administered and there was a discussion about taking Lynn to Theatre to try and get control of the bleeding but, in the end, they had to admit defeat.

Someone looked up at the clock on the wall. 'Time of death,' they said quietly. 'Sixteen forty-three...'

Lynn Grimshaw had tragically become one of the very rare cases of a woman dying during childbirth even in a well-equipped hospital setting.

The silence that followed the announcement of the time of death only lasted a few seconds but it was one of the most profound silences Jenni had ever experienced.

Even the tiny baby in the room was quiet. And still.

Everyone was still. Maybe that was why Jenni was suddenly aware of her own babies moving.

It was then that a new fear was born.

What if something terrible happened when *she* was giving birth?

Alone...?

What if her babies survived but there was no one there to hold them?

Like...their *father*...?

CHAPTER ELEVEN

BETWEEN THE INTERNAL hospital driveway and the main road leading into the centre of the town there was a garden that was the pride and joy of the Picton Hospital groundsmen.

There was a central fountain, neatly clipped hedges, rose gardens bursting with colour in the summer, shelter from the huge horse chestnut trees and plenty of rustic wooden benches to provide seating. It was popular with staff members, visitors and patients who were mobile enough to escape outside for a break and a bit of fresh air on fine days.

It was usually easy to find an empty bench that afforded privacy, which meant it was also a refuge for people who needed time and space alone to deal with the unimaginable, and when Dan went looking for Jenni as the traumatic aftermath of a totally unexpected patient death was finally ebbing, someone told him that they'd seen her going into the garden a short time ago.

It was dark outside now and while there were

antique-style streetlamps that provided plenty of light, it didn't seem a safe place for a woman to be alone. It would also be cold. Dan picked up one of the hospital's bright red woollen blankets before he went out to see if Jenni was still there. If she wasn't, he was going to find her.

He'd seen the fear in her eyes when the call had been made to stop Lynn's resuscitation and her time of death had been recorded.

She was due to give birth herself in a matter of weeks and she'd just witnessed the worst possible outcome.

She couldn't be alone.

She might not want his company but Dan knew that Jock and Grace were still out of town and... he couldn't let her be alone...

Because he loved her.

He found her, sitting alone near the very centre of the garden. She wasn't crying but she looked so forlorn that Dan could actually feel his heart cracking. She was also shivering so, without saying anything, Dan wrapped her in the fuzzy red blanket.

And then he sat down beside her and wrapped her in his arms.

Oh...

Grace had been so right, hadn't she?

Home *could* be a person and not a place.

She should have known that all along. Jenni

hadn't felt this afraid since she was a child, and in those days it had been Jock who could make her feel safe.

She was grown up now and confident enough in her independence that she'd been more than happy to plan on being a single parent. But she couldn't make herself feel quite *this* safe. Because the love that wrapped around you from the outside was so very powerful—if you could trust it.

But how could you trust anything when it felt like everything that mattered the most was teetering on the edge of a cliff?

'I'm scared,' she whispered against his chest. 'I'm *so* scared, Dan.'

'I know.' He held her tighter. 'It's not going to happen to you, Jen.'

'It happened to Lynn.' Jenni could feel tears that had been caught by the ache in her chest for hours and hours beginning to escape. 'Why…? *How* did that happen? Did I miss something that could have stopped it happening?'

'No.' The word was certain. 'There were discussions about it when you went with Chris and the baby to NICU for her neonatal check. The general consensus is that it was most likely an amniotic fluid embolism. She had all the features, with an acute maternal collapse and foetal compromise during labour or immediately after the birth. She had the respiratory symptoms, hypotension, confusion, agitation…'

'But the bleeding... Did we miss an abruption?'

'They think the bleeding was caused by coagulopathy. Clotting issues also fit the preliminary diagnosis. We'll know more after the post-mortem.' Dan's breath came out in a sigh. 'You and Maria did as well as you could have done. I hear the baby's doing well. They're only going to keep her under observation in NICU overnight.'

'Chris isn't leaving her side. He even took her with him when he was taken to see Lynn.' The tears were flowing faster now. 'I went with him. He told her that he was going to look after their daughter for the rest of his life. That he would always love her...twice as much as he would have because he'd make sure she had her mother's love as well. That he was going to love her as much as he's always loved Lynn...'

Jenni's voice broke completely. Dan tried to say something but the words were too strangled so Jenni scrubbed at her face and tried again.

'I was going to go back to Scotland the day after tomorrow,' she confessed. 'I've got the tickets and everything.'

'No...' The word was almost a plea. 'Please don't do that, Jen. I don't want to lose you...'

'I'm not going to do it,' she said. 'I knew I couldn't the moment Lynn died. When I saw her baby in her father's arms. You have to be there, Dan...in case something bad happens to me...'

'Nothing bad is going to happen.' Dan had his

cheek pressed against Jenni's hair. 'I won't let it. I'll keep you safe… I'll keep you *all* safe…'

They both knew that was a promise that couldn't be made, but it was what Jenni needed to hear.

'Even if you don't believe that you're their father?'

'But I do,' Dan said.

Jenni shifted in his arms, sitting up enough to be able to see his face properly. 'But…'

'I said it badly,' Dan said quietly. 'What I meant was that even if I wasn't their father biologically, I would still feel like I am.' Jenni could hear him pulling in a deep breath. 'And that's been the hardest thing for me—a risk I never thought I could ever take again. To have the dream of being a father come true and then to lose it.'

'*Again…?*' Jenni felt a shiver run down her spine. 'I knew you'd been married but you never said you'd lost a child. You said you *couldn't* have kids…'

Her brain was trying—and failing—to fit puzzle pieces together.

'I believed I was going to become a father.' Dan was speaking slowly, his tone bleak. 'My wife found out she was pregnant, ironically not long after we'd had the results of my first fertility test, when we were just starting to gather information about using technology to try and help us start a family.'

'So you knew it wasn't impossible…' Jenni wasn't sure if she'd spoken those words aloud but Dan seemed to be responding to them.

'She let me believe I'd beaten those astronomical odds for months but then I found out about the affair she'd been having for the last year. That the father of her baby was actually the man that she ended up leaving me to be with.'

The puzzle pieces were falling into place with painful precision.

Jenni could hear echoes of things that Dan had said on the evening they'd met for the first time.

'If you trust someone who tells you lies, you give them the power to destroy you…'

'Fool me once, shame on you. Fool me twice, shame on me…'

Jenni sat up straighter. She lifted her hand to place it on Dan's cheek. 'I get it,' she said softly. 'And I'm sorry. I was asking too much.'

She could feel Dan shaking his head beneath her hand. He opened his mouth to say something, but Jenni shifted her hand so that her fingers were on his lips to prevent any words escaping. She had more she wanted to say first.

'I expected you to believe me simply because I knew I was telling the truth. I wish I'd known what you just told me because then I would have known that you didn't have that kind of trust any longer, and I *know* what that's like. Do you remember me telling you that Jock and I made a vow when we were thirteen that we'd never get married because we saw our mother bounce from one marriage or relationship to the next and they never turned out well?'

This time Jenni could feel the nod beneath her hand but she still didn't move her fingers.

'There's something I didn't tell you, though. I didn't tell you that Jock and I learned that it was better not to trust even the people that said they loved you—maybe *especially* those people—because they made you hope that things would be different, but it never lasted. We learned not to trust before we even understood what trust was.' She swallowed hard. 'And we learned that it was always our fault. That just being born had ruined our mum's life, so it wasn't her fault that she never kept her promises. The ones about Father Christmas bringing presents or that she'd be there to see our school play didn't matter so much. The worst were the ones she made when she'd fallen in love—yet again—and promised us that everything was going to be wonderful because we'd be a real family this time. Years before we made the vow about not getting married or having kids, Jock told me he was never, ever going to make a promise he couldn't keep and I said I was never going to tell lies. Jock said that a broken promise was a kind of lie, but it felt bigger to me.'

Jenni was trying to smile but her lips wouldn't cooperate. 'Do you remember when I told you, that night we first met, that I never lie and you asked how you could know whether that was a lie?'

Her fingers had slipped away from Dan's lips now but he didn't say anything. He just gave a slow single nod.

'*That's* why,' Jenni said. 'I can't deliberately lie because I know how much it can hurt. That's why I understand why it's been so hard for you to trust—in me, in relationships…in a universe that's made something happen that's magic because you never thought it could happen. But it's the truth, Dan, and…and so is this…' Jenni took a very deep breath. 'Up until now in my life, Jock's been the only person I've trusted enough to love with all my heart. I never thought I'd trust anyone else that much. Or love anyone else this much, but I love you, Daniel Walker. That much and more. And I love our babies. *Our* babies…' She found the smile she'd lost. 'You're the only person I've slept with in more than a year.' Her voice dropped to a whisper. 'You're the only person I *want* to sleep with for the rest of my life…'

'That's exactly how long I want you in my bed,' Dan said softly. 'How good is that?' He bent his head to brush her lips with his own. 'I thought I couldn't believe in miracles any longer. That I couldn't even believe in love. But you've changed everything. And we've been reminded today that life can change in a heartbeat. *This* is what really matters.'

He pressed a real kiss onto Jenni's lips this time and then rested his forehead against hers. 'I love you,' he said. 'I think I fell in love with you that first night. When you told me you can sleep like a starfish. I just didn't realise that it had happened—until the day of Jock and Grace's wedding. It took me a few days to find the courage to tell you and...well...that didn't turn out so well, did it?'

'That was my fault more than yours. I'm sorry...'

'I get it. And I was asking too much from you, wasn't I? That I could tell you that I love you but, at the same time, tell you that I still couldn't believe the impossible had happened and I was the babies' father.'

The echo of her own words about asking too much just made this soul-deep connection between them stronger.

And she could hear another echo. The question of whether she could trust the love she could feel all around her.

The love that was coming from Dan.

That was the moment she knew she *could* trust it. It felt like she had no choice because she loved Dan. She had already given him her heart.

And he was still holding her as if that was exactly what he wanted. As if he loved *her* that much.

Maybe he could feel what she was thinking.

'I love you,' Dan told her again, softly. 'I need to be this close to you…for ever…' But he broke the contact of their skin a moment later. 'Come home with me now,' he said. 'I want to take care of you and it's too cold out here.'

It *was* cold. Jenni's legs felt stiff as she got to her feet. Her whole body felt stiff, in fact. And sore enough to make her groan.

'What's wrong?'

'I think I've done something to my back. It's really sore…'

Dan put one hand on her lower back. 'Here?'

'Yes.'

Dan's other hand was on her belly. 'Can you feel that?'

Of course she could. The tightening was like a vice being wound up. 'It's a contraction,' she said. 'I've had Braxton Hicks contractions before. It'll go in a few seconds.'

Except it didn't.

Her belly had never become this hard before. Hard enough to make the pain in her back become more intense.

The fear and distress that had brought Jenni into the sanctuary of this garden in the first place had begun to fade the moment Dan had taken her into his arms. As they'd opened their hearts to each other the connection between them had felt strong enough to conquer anything.

But the fear was crowding in again.

The fear that something terrible was going to happen and all the love in the world couldn't prevent it.

'I think this is a *real* contraction.' Jenni's voice was hollow. 'And it's too early.' She met Dan's gaze. She didn't need to tell him how scared she was. She could see a reflection of her own fear in his eyes.

He pulled the fuzzy red blanket around her more tightly and then lifted her into his arms as if she wasn't such an awkward, heavy shape with her huge belly.

'I've got you,' he said as he began to walk back towards the hospital. 'We've got this… Just hang on.'

Jenni wrapped her arms around his neck and held on.

As tightly as she could.

Maria Gould was still the obstetrician on call for Picton Hospital that evening and she arrived in a commendably short period of time after Dan strode into the emergency department with Jenni in his arms.

'How long have you been getting the contractions?'

'I'm not sure. I've had a few Braxton Hicks contractions over the last week or two but I wasn't really paying much attention earlier.'

Maria nodded. She knew exactly why. 'It's been a very stressful day,' she said quietly. 'And you've been on your feet for a long time.

Jenni tried to hold back the wave of fear. 'Severe stress is a known cause for preterm labour, isn't it? And carrying twins is another.'

Had Dan sensed how frightened she was? Was that why he took hold of her hand? Maria wasn't the only staff member in this resuscitation room she'd been put in. The news that they were in a relationship was going to spread like wildfire, but maybe Dan sensed that thought as well and that was why he gave her hand a reassuring squeeze.

He wasn't going to let anything stop him staying this close to her.

'This is only a suspected PTL,' Maria said calmly. 'It's not established yet. Have your waters broken?'

'No.'

'Any bleeding or discharge?'

'No. But I've had a sore back for a while.'

'Yes, I remember you saying this morning that you were getting backache quite often.' If this experienced consultant was feeling justified in having been reluctant to give Jenni clearance to take an international flight back to Scotland she was professional enough not to let it show. 'Is this pain different? Worse?'

'It gets more intense when I'm getting a contraction.'

'How often are they happening?'

Jenni looked up at Dan, who was standing right beside her bed. 'She's had two in the last ten minutes or so.'

Maria nodded. 'We'll get continuous CTG monitoring on for you and see what the frequency and duration of these contractions are. Stress is a known trigger for increased Braxton Hicks activity. I'm going to do an ultrasound to have a look at your cervix to see if there's any indication of thinning or dilating and we'll go from there.'

Jenni nodded but it was Dan's gaze she sought as the anchor she needed.

'We've got this, darling,' he said.

Both his tone and the endearment made it clear that he wasn't simply holding Jenni's hand as a friend. Maria had a little more difficulty in hiding her reaction this time. A hint of a smile was there now.

'We *have* got this,' she said. 'I'm going to get some air transport on standby just in case we do need to transfer you to a facility with a higher level of neonatal intensive care available, like Wellington or Christchurch. We can give you tocolytic drugs to slow or stop a premature labour if that's what's actually happening and we'd also give you steroids to lower the risks for the babies of any complications for preterm birth.'

A portable ultrasound machine was being

wheeled into the room. The CTG machine was right behind it.

'Has someone let Jock know what's going on?' Maria asked as the technician got ready to place transducers on Jenni's belly.

'I can do that,' Dan offered.

This time Maria let herself smile warmly. 'No. Don't move,' she said. 'I think you're in exactly the right place at the moment. I'll go and give Jock a quick call before I do the ultrasound.'

Jock and Grace were in the room when Maria visited the maternity ward later the next day.

'How did you get back so fast?' she asked them.

'We were already on the way,' Jock said. 'That's why I didn't pick up your message for a while.' He was smiling at his twin sister. 'Talk about coming down to earth with a bump. The honeymoon is definitely over.'

'Sorry about that,' Maria said. 'I should have waited before calling anyway. I hear things have settled nicely overnight, so it seems that this has been a false alarm and the combination of Braxton Hicks, backache and the involvement in a traumatic case was enough to give us all a fright.'

'I heard about Lynn…' Grace had tears in her eyes. 'It's so awful…'

Jock put his arm around Grace's shoulders but it was Jenni whose gaze he was holding. 'A once in a lifetime event in your career, I hope,' he said.

'But the worst time it could have happened. I'm sorry I wasn't here.'

'You're here now,' Jenni said. 'And…it was okay because… Dan was here.'

Dan reached for her hand but spoke to Jock and Grace. 'I've been up to NICU this morning. The baby's fine. The dad, Chris, has a hugely supportive family, including his in-laws, who are surrounding him. He's still in shock, of course, but he told me that this is the way he can honour his wife—by protecting their child—and he's not going to let either of them down.'

They were all quiet for a long moment, which made it easy to hear the sound of two strong foetal hearts beating in the background.

'I think we can take those transducers off,' Maria said. 'And let you go home to rest properly. As long as you've got someone keeping a close eye on you?'

'I'll be doing that,' Dan said.

'So will we,' Grace added, sharing a glance with Jock.

Maria was giving Jenni a stern look now. 'I'll want to see you every few days from now on. We'll be doing a biophysical profile ultrasound at least once a week. You do realise there's absolutely no chance of you getting on any international flights now, don't you?'

'What?' Grace and Jock spoke together.

'Long story,' Jenni told them. 'I'll tell you later.'

She smiled at Maria. 'It's okay, I'm not planning to go anywhere. I'll be cancelling my tickets first thing in the morning.'

'You're coming home with us,' Jock said. 'I'm not having you alone in that hospital accommodation.'

'No...' Dan shook his head. 'She's coming home with me.'

Everybody was looking at Jenni.

She was looking at Dan.

'I will come home with you, please,' she said softly. Her smile was wry. 'Good thing I have all my things pretty much packed already.'

Maria was looking from Jenni to Dan and back to Jenni. 'When did this all start?' she asked. 'When you stepped in for Grace and began working here?'

'Um...' Jenni shared a glance with Dan. Asking permission to share something private? The smile she received looked like permission. 'We actually met a while ago,' she told Maria. 'Around the time I got pregnant.'

'At exactly the time she got pregnant,' Dan added. 'I'm the father of these babies.'

Maria's jaw dropped.

'That reminds me,' Jenni said. 'I need to get some blood taken for a DNA test. We might need to provide proof of Dan's paternity for the twins' birth certificates. The powers-that-be might be justified in being a bit suspicious of someone arriving in the country already pregnant and then claiming citizenship for their kids.'

'Well, I never...' Maria seemed lost for words. She looked at Dan and then at Jock. She shook her head. 'I should have known that things were going to change around here when your twin arrived. Double trouble...' She gave Jenni another stern look but she was smiling at the same time. 'No more trouble with this pregnancy, though, thank you. You go home and take it easy. Your job is to keep those babies inside for as long as you can. Two or three weeks would be ideal.'

It was exactly three weeks later when Dan arrived home from work to find Jenni slowly pacing the floor, her hand pressed against her back.

'Backache again?'

She nodded.

'Any contractions?'

'Just the usual Braxton Hicks. I'm counting. I've only had two in the last thirty minutes.'

Dan shrugged off his jacket and hooked it over a chair beside the dining table. He put his phone down on the table and picked up an envelope lying beside a bowl of fruit. 'What's this?'

'It came today.'

'Looks official.' Dan scanned the return address and his jaw dropped as his gaze locked with Jenni's. 'It's from the laboratory in Wellington. It's the DNA test results.'

'I know…'

'You haven't opened it.'

'I thought we should do that together.'

Dan nodded but his mouth had gone very dry and his fingers wouldn't move. And then the envelope slipped from his fingers to land back on the table and become irrelevant for the moment because Jenni had suddenly wrapped her arms around her belly and was leaning forward. Fluid was running down her legs to puddle on the wooden floor.

'My waters have broken.' Her announcement was redundant. 'Or one of them, at least. Maybe they're not just Braxton Hicks.' Her eyes were wide. 'They're not painful but we'd better start timing them.'

'Maria wants you in hospital at the first sign of labour.' Dan's heart rate had picked up noticeably. 'As far as I'm concerned, your waters breaking is right up near the top of that list.'

'Ooh…' Jenni was hanging on to the back of the couch now. 'Okay… I can feel this one…'

'I'll get your bag. Are you all right there for a sec?'

'Yes. Can you get a towel for the car too?'

'Don't move. I'll be right back.'

Jenni had packed her hospital bag ages ago— during the first days after she'd been released from monitoring the premature labour scare they'd had. When she had moved in with Dan and they were sharing the bubble of being openly in love and totally committed to each other.

Those days had passed in a dreamy blur for Dan.

There was, of course, no hint of anything sexual in their relationship currently but, strangely, that had made it deeper and so much more intense. They had lain in bed together, holding hands and…talking. Talking for hours and hours, night after night. They'd shared memories of their childhoods, the minefield of being teenagers, tales of failed relationships and the passion of training and working in their chosen careers. They knew each other's favourite foods and music and movies, books they'd choose to read again and places they'd love to travel to.

They knew each other now—it was as simple as that.

They loved each other—it was as significant as that.

And they were about to become parents together—and it was as life-changing as that.

Dan had the handles of a soft bag over his shoulder and those of a larger bag in his hand as he got back to the open-plan living area. Jenni had ignored his instruction to not move and was heading for the door. Dan increased his stride to catch up, but had to pause as he noticed his phone on the table. He reached to pick it up and for some reason he also picked up the envelope beside it that he'd dropped only minutes ago. He stuffed both items into the side pocket of the bag over his shoulder.

'Wait for me,' he called as Jenni disappeared through the door. 'Don't go trying to get down those stairs by yourself.'

It was only a fifteen-minute drive to get to the hospital but Jenni had to cope with five contractions, each of them lasting forty-five to sixty seconds. Dan was trying to hold Jenni's hand when she reached for him and at the same time trying to drive safely and swiftly with only one hand on the wheel. It was a relief for both of them when he turned into the ambulance bay and abandoned the car to run inside and grab a wheelchair. Other staff members rushed to help and Jenni saw Dan throw his car keys towards an orderly so that someone else could sort shifting the vehicle.

It wasn't just Maria waiting for them in the labour suite. As her midwife, Grace was there and either she or Dan must have called Jock because he was there as well. Looking excited but nervous.

'You can't come in,' Jenni told her brother.

'No, you can't.' Grace backed her up. 'You'll have to wait outside because Jenni doesn't want you to see her lady bits.'

'But I see them all the time,' Jock protested.

'Not mine, you don't.'

'Sorry, mate.' Dan threw a look over his shoulder as he pushed Jenni's wheelchair into the room. 'I'll keep you posted, I promise.'

'Oh, I've got the penthouse suite,' Jenni said. 'How did you manage that, Grace?'

'Pure luck it wasn't occupied when Dan rang,' Grace said. 'I ran up and put dibs on it for you. I've even started filling the pool.'

Jenni felt the wheelchair stop but she couldn't move to get out of it. She was gripped by a new contraction and the increase in intensity—and pain—had, quite literally, stolen her breath away.

'Remember to breathe…' Grace's calm voice was close to her ear. 'You've got this, Jen.'

Jenni managed to blow out a breath.

'Forty-five seconds.' Grace clicked a stopwatch. 'Can we get you on the bed so that Maria can give you the once-over and see how far along you are?'

Jenni wasn't at all sure she wanted to stay on the bed, however, especially when Maria told her she was six centimetres dilated and in active labour. Another contraction had started only two minutes after the last and this one was painful enough to make her groan.

'Have you changed your mind about preferences for pain relief?' Maria asked. 'Are you still wanting to avoid an epidural?'

'Not unless it's needed for a Caesarean,' Jenni said. 'Can I try a hot shower first, Grace?'

'Of course. The pool's nearly ready too, if you still fancy being in water.'

The shower helped but it was sinking into the warmth of the deep water in the birthing pool later that made a real difference.

'This feels amazing,' Jenni sighed. She knelt in the pool, her arms hooked over the side. Dan knelt on the floor in front of her, his hands on her arms.

Her contractions were speeding up and getting longer. When she felt ready to push, Maria put on long plastic gloves that went up to her elbows so that she could check on how dilated her cervix was.

'You're good to go,' she told Jenni. Then she turned to Dan. 'Do you want to get in the pool with her?'

'Can I?'

'Yes.'

'I put boxer shorts in the bag for you,' Jenni told him. 'In case you wanted to.'

'Do you want me to?'

'Yes… I need you closer.'

She sat back in the pool as soon as Dan climbed in, so that she could lean against him within the circle of his arms. She could push back on him to brace herself and he could push back against her for more support and it felt as if they were both bringing this first baby into the world.

Grace was on one side of the pool and Maria on the other.

'You're doing so well, Jen,' Grace said. 'Keep pushing. Gentle pushes now…keep going…that's it…and breathe…'

'Baby's head's out,' Maria said. 'Wait for the next contraction…'

It came within seconds. Jenni barely had time to reach down to feel her baby's head.

'Big push…' Grace sounded breathless herself. 'Keep it up…there we are…'

Twin A—their baby boy—was lifted from the water to be put on Jenni's chest, still within the circle of Dan's arms. For a long, long moment, it felt like it was just the three of them because Grace and Maria somehow managed to fade into the background. Jenni had done that herself, so many times, as she'd witnessed this magic time when a new family was born, but she'd had no idea how powerful it actually was until she was holding her own infant and looked up to see her own emotions reflected in the eyes of the man she loved.

But the water was getting cold now and she shivered.

'The cord's stopped pulsing,' Maria said. 'Would you like to cut it, Dan?'

'Yes…' Dan took the scissors after the clamps were in place. Jenni was still shivering and had goosebumps on her arms.

'We need to get you out of the pool,' Grace said. 'It's too cold.'

Jenni squeezed her eyes shut. 'I'm not sure I want to do this again.'

She could hear the smile in her best friend's voice. 'You're already doing it,' Grace said.

Dan climbed out first and Grace wrapped the baby for him to hold but then, as Jenni was helped to climb onto the bed, she got the most intense contraction yet and cried out for him.

'Your waters have just broken for Baby B,' Grace said.

'And she's managed to turn herself around,' Maria added. 'I can see her foot.'

Jenni was shocked. Their baby girl was now a footling breech and she felt a flash of fear. 'I need you, Dan,' she called. 'I need you to hold me again...'

'But...'

Dan was torn. He looked down at the tiny face of his oh, so vulnerable premature newborn son. Then he looked at the face of the woman he loved, twisted by pain and fear, and the decision was a no-brainer. He made an executive decision and he opened the door of the birthing suite.

'Jock? Get in here. You need to hold your nephew for a minute or two.'

A minute was pretty much all it took for Twin B's somewhat dramatic entrance into the world to be completed and this time the parents were dry and warm as they cuddled their daughter and waited to cut the cord.

Jock brought the little boy back to join his family. 'I didn't see a thing,' he assured Jenni.

She smiled but there were tears lurking. Such happy tears.

She had her entire family here. Jock and Grace, Dan and these two beautiful, healthy babies. They would need a thorough paediatric check very soon and would probably need to spend a day or two in the NICU, but they were doing well enough for Maria to deem the parents could have a few minutes to themselves when it was all over and there were no signs of any problems with either Jenni or the babies.

Everyone else left the room.

Dan adjusted the pillows on either side of Jenni so that she had a baby in the crook of each arm.

'Look at them,' he said softly. 'They're perfect...just like you... I love you, Jenni McKay. Too much to be able to find the words. Mind you, I've never been that great at finding words...'

He leaned closer to kiss her, so tenderly it made her heart ache.

'You found some pretty good words,' she murmured. 'I love you too, Daniel Walker.' She looked from one baby to the other. 'And you're right... these guys *are* perfect.'

'I'll just get my phone,' Dan said. 'I need a picture of this.'

He delved into the pocket of the bag to find his phone and Jenni saw an envelope fall to the floor at the same time.

'What's that?'

'Nothing…' Dan snatched it up and went to put it back into the bag. 'I don't know why I even picked it up when we left home.'

'It's the DNA paternity test results, isn't it?'

'Yes.'

'Bring it here.'

'Why?'

'I want to see it.'

'I don't,' Dan said.

'Don't you?'

'No.'

'Why not?'

'Because I don't need to,' Dan said quietly. 'I already know I'm the twins' father.'

Jenni knew exactly what would be on that result sheet but she still wanted to see it—in black and white—officially recorded for ever.

'Humour me.' Jenni smiled. 'I've just given birth.'

Dan had to open the envelope and pull out the sheet of paper to give to Jenni because she could only use one hand. He kept his eyes on the twins as she scanned the contents. The silence finally made him look up. He swallowed hard as he saw the tears in Jenni's eyes.

'Do I want to know?' he asked softly.

This time, her smile was so full of love it lit up the whole room.

'You were right,' she whispered. 'You already know.'

EPILOGUE

Two years later...

THE BRIDESMAID WAS heavily pregnant.

'I'm so happy that my bridesmaid's dress is getting a second outing,' Jenni said.

Grace patted her belly. 'I'm so happy that I've only got one baby in here. I don't know how you've coped so well with twins. There... I think we're finished here.' She used a final hairpin to secure the half-updo she'd given Jenni that left a tumble of red curls to tickle the bare top of her back. 'You look absolutely gorgeous.'

Jenni stood up and did a twirl in the living area of the small cottage they were in, getting ready for this wedding. 'I can't believe I found the perfect dress in a shop in Blenheim. A vintage nineteen-forties dress, even.'

The pale mushroom silk and lace dress had a fitted bodice with a sweetheart neckline, tiny cap sleeves and a swing skirt that had a ballerina length hem. Like Grace had done when she'd married Jock more than two years earlier, she was wearing only flowers in her hair for this intimate wedding ceremony that they'd chosen to have at Furneaux Lodge, a beautiful historic homestead at the head of Endeavor Inlet in the Marlborough Sounds that had a backdrop of native bush and only well-kept lawns between the homestead and the beach. Just out of sight, moored on glassy smooth water, was Jock's boat *Lassie* that had brought them all out into the Sounds a couple of days ago.

Jock and Grace were in one of the resort's self-contained cottages—right beside the one that Jenni and Dan and the twins were in. Both cottages had a view across the lawns to the beach and the two friends took a moment to look out and soak in the blues and greens of a perfect New Zealand summer's afternoon.

'Brilliant idea, this,' Grace said. 'To have your wedding and honeymoon in the same place.' Then she laughed. 'And to invite the rest of your family to stay as well.'

'You need a babymoon,' Jenni told her. 'You won't have any time for much of a holiday for ages after that baby of yours turns up.'

'You got to go to Scotland. How old were the twins then? Nine months?'

'Aye…but I wouldn't recommend international travel with two babies. We only did that because I needed to sort all the legal stuff to sell my house and tie up all the loose ends so we could get on with finding our new house in Picton.'

They didn't have a private beach and a jetty like Jock and Grace did. They'd found an old villa on the hill, very like the hospital accommodation that had been a part of both Jenni and Grace's journey to finding the men they would be spending the rest of their lives with.

Their loves...

'Oh, look...' Grace was shading her eyes as she peered down at the beach.

'Are they building sandcastles?'

There were two tall men on the beach already, their trouser legs and the sleeves of their white shirts rolled up as they did their best to keep two excited toddlers entertained until the bride arrived. Their celebrant, Aroha, was waiting patiently near an archway that had been positioned on the beach, ready to frame the bride and groom as they exchanged vows against the stunning backdrop of one of the most beautiful places in the world.

'That'll be Dan's idea. I would have gone for collecting some shells myself.' But Jenni's smile was misty. 'He's the best dad ever. I'm so lucky...'

'He thinks he's even luckier. I heard him tell Jock that the other night when they were having that two-man stag party at our place. I'm just surprised it took him more than two years to propose to you.'

'He didn't,' Jenni confessed. 'I proposed to *him*.'

'Really?' Grace blinked.

'Really. I don't think he would ever have proposed. He knew I had no intention of ever getting married and he said it didn't matter—that all he wanted was for us to be together. For ever...'

'Oh...that's so romantic.'

'I had the feeling that he wanted to be married, though. Deep down. When you and Jock told us you were having a baby, he made a joke about Jock breaking both the vows we'd made when we were teenagers. Up to then we'd only broken half of them—one each—with him getting married and me having kids. There was something in his voice that caught me...here...' Jenni touched the skin over her heart. 'So that's when I proposed. I said I wanted to tell the world how much I love him and what an incredible father he is...to wear his ring for the rest of my life and to see him wearing mine.'

Grace was looking misty herself now. 'Come on...let's get down there. I want to hear these vows and see you both putting those rings on each other's fingers. And I want to see Sophie and Noah throwing rose petals at their parents— if they're not building sandcastles again by then.'

Jenni swallowed back tears of joy that might well ruin her eye make-up. There would be time for those later, perhaps, when she was folded into Dan's arms much later tonight. For now, there were declarations of love and promises to share with the people that mattered the most in the world.

With her family…

And, most of all, with the love of her life.

He was waiting for her on the beach. She saw him look up, as if he was wondering how soon he might see her.

Jenni gathered the ripples of her skirt in her hands and looked over her shoulder at Grace. 'Come on… I can't wait any longer…'

* * * * *